American Soul

The Contested Legacy of the *Declaration of Independence*

Edited with an Introduction by
Justin Buckley Dyer

Foreword by
David L. Boren

Published by Rowman & Littlefield
A wholly owned subsidiary of The Rowman & Littlefield Publishing Group, Inc.
4501 Forbes Boulevard, Suite 200, Lanham, Maryland 20706
www.rowman.com

Unit A, Whitacre Mews, 26-34 Stannary Street, London SE11 4AB

Copyright © 2012 by Rowman & Littlefield Publishers, Inc.
First paperback edition 2015

All rights reserved. No part of this book may be reproduced in any form or by any electronic or mechanical means, including information storage and retrieval systems, without written permission from the publisher, except by a reviewer who may quote passages in a review.

British Library Cataloguing in Publication Information Available

Library of Congress Cataloging-in-Publication Data

The hardback edition of this book was previously cataloged by the Library of Congress as follows:

American soul : the contested legacy of the Declaration of Independence / edited with an introduction by Justin Buckley Dyer, foreword by David L. Boren.
   p. cm.
 Includes bibliographical references and index.
 1. United States. Declaration of Independence. 2. United States. Declaration of Independence—Criticism, Textual. I. Dyer, Justin B.
   E221.A48 2011
   973.3'13—dc23   2011027813

ISBN 978-1-4422-1146-9 (cloth : alk. paper)
ISBN 978-1-4422-1147-6 (pbk. : alk. paper)
ISBN 978-1-4422-1148-3 (electronic : alk. paper)

∞™ The paper used in this publication meets the minimum requirements of American National Standard for Information Sciences—Permanence of Paper for Printed Library Materials, ANSI/NISO Z39.48-1992.

Printed in the United States of America

First comes the Declaration of Independence, the illuminated letter of our history. . . . Here is the national heart, the national soul, the national will, the national voice, which must inspire our interpretation of the Constitution, and enter into and diffuse itself through all the national legislation.

—Charles Sumner, 1860

Contents

Acknowledgments	ix
Foreword *David L. Boren*	xi
Introduction	xv

Part I: The Declaration and the American Founding

1	The Declaration of Independence *Continental Congress, 1776*	3
2	Rough Draft of the Declaration of Independence *Thomas Jefferson, 1776*	7
3	Letters to Abigail *John Adams, 1776*	12
4	A Short Review of the Declaration *Jeremy Bentham, 1776*	16
5	The American Mind *Thomas Jefferson, 1825*	19
6	Popular Sovereignty *James Wilson, 1787*	20
7	Keeping the Revolution *Daniel Webster, 1802*	22

8	The American and French Revolutions *Lemuel Shaw, 1815*	26
9	American Principles *John Quincy Adams, 1821*	30
10	Fifty Years Later *Thomas Jefferson, 1826*	34
11	The Lives and Characters of Thomas Jefferson and John Adams *William Wirt, 1826*	36

Part II: The Declaration in a House Divided

12	Petition for Freedom *"A Great Number of Blackes," 1777*	43
13	The Constitution and Slavery *Luther Martin, 1787*	45
14	Republican Consistency! *William Lloyd Garrison, 1838*	49
15	*Amistad* Argument *John Quincy Adams, 1841*	53
16	The Cause of the Present Crisis *John C. Calhoun, 1848*	58
17	What to the Slave is the Fourth of July? *Frederick Douglass, 1852*	63
18	Party Platform *Republican National Convention, 1856*	68
19	The *Dred Scott* Decision *Chief Justice Roger Taney, 1857*	70
20	Debate on the *Dred Scott* Decision *Abraham Lincoln and Stephen Douglas, 1858*	74
21	The Chief Cornerstone *Alexander Stephens, 1861*	79
22	Gettysburg Address *Abraham Lincoln, 1863*	83
23	Reconstructing America *United States Congress, 1864–1870*	85

Contents vii

Part III: The Declaration in the Modern World

24	Seneca Falls Declaration *Elizabeth Cady Stanton and Lucretia Mott, 1848*	93
25	Declaration of the Rights of Women *National Woman Suffrage Association, 1876*	98
26	The Inevitability of Women's Suffrage *Carrie Chapman Catt, 1917*	103
27	What is Progress? *Woodrow Wilson, 1913*	107
28	Speech on the Fourth of July *Calvin Coolidge, 1926*	112
29	Commonwealth Club Address *Franklin Roosevelt, 1932*	121
30	Speech at the Bicentennial of the Constitution *Thurgood Marshall, 1987*	129
31	The Sanctity of Human Life *Ronald Reagan, 1984*	134
32	America's Work in the World *George W. Bush, 2003*	136
33	A More Perfect Union *Barack Obama, 2008*	139
Notes		149
Index		155
About the Author		157

Acknowledgments

The groundwork for this project was laid several years ago as I was working on my doctoral dissertation at the University of Texas. While studying the development of American antislavery constitutionalism, I discovered that appeals to the Declaration by antislavery jurists and statesmen had been ubiquitous in the nineteenth century. What particularly grabbed my attention, however, was the degree to which arguments about the "Laws of Nature and Nature's God" had structured the antebellum debate over slavery in America. My initial interest in natural law and the politics of slavery pointed, as well, to broader questions about the Declaration and the American constitutional tradition.

Texas provided an ideal intellectual environment to study such things. In conversations with professors and colleagues, often over a pint of beer, I was challenged to think about the meaning (and perhaps radical implications) of the Declaration, the relationship between classical and modern natural law theories, and the proper place of natural law arguments in contemporary American politics. The debts I amassed are numerous, but I would especially like to thank Gary Jacobsohn, J. Budziszewski, Kevin Stuart, Kody Cooper, and Matthew Wright. Its been said that the worst part about attending graduate school in Austin is having to leave when you are done. Good friends and good mentors made this all the more true for me.

Still, after leaving Texas I could have wished for nothing better than to settle in at the University of Missouri. Warm and intellectually engaging students and colleagues have made it difficult to call what I do on a day-to-day basis "work." I am also indebted to the institutional support I have received, and I would like to thank Jonathan Cisco and Seulhan Lee, in particular, for helpful assistance tracking down and compiling the documents for this volume.

The second, paperback edition of *American Soul* is part of a larger project supported by the Jack Miller Center for Teaching America's Founding Principles and History and made possible by a generous grant from the Kinder Foundation, a family foundation established by Rich and Nancy Kinder. Recently, the Miller Center was instrumental in the establishment at the University of Missouri of the Kinder Forum on Constitutional Democracy, an interdisciplinary program devoted to excellence in teaching and scholarship about American constitutional democracy. It is heartening to see a renewed interest in the foundations of American constitutional government at institutions of higher education in the United States. As David Boren writes in his foreword, "We must renew our determination to pass on our national story to the next generation." There is a lot of work to be done, and I am excited that the University of Missouri is positioned to contribute in significant ways to that ongoing project.

Foreword

David L. Boren

In this book, Justin Dyer has given us an in-depth look into the history and impact of the Declaration of Independence. Through primary resources, including Thomas Jefferson's original draft of the Declaration, he examines how world leaders have interpreted this historical document and what we can still learn from it.

The great historian David McCullough once said that in order for our nation to be great we must learn how it became great in the first place. We cannot preserve and give life to the precious documents like the Declaration of Independence and the United States Constitution unless we know what they say and why they were was drafted as they were.

The United States is dramatically a different kind of nation than when the Declaration was written. Many Americans are immigrants or children of immigrants, are of varied races, adhere to different religions, and have richly diverse cultural backgrounds. We come not from one place but from all places. What makes our government and our people is a great experiment that continues to be tested today. What makes us Americans is not a common tribal identity. Instead, it is our common set of values and a shared commitment to the political institutions that preserve them.

We cannot intelligently participate in the current debates about the limits of governmental power and the importance of the independent judicial process unless we understand our history. James Madison was right when he said, "The diffusion of knowledge is the only true guardian of liberty."

For each of us, it is our life story that gives us our identity. What we have experienced—our personal histories— define us. To lose your personal story is to lose your personhood. The same is true for our national story.

If we forget it, we lose our vision, our identity, and our national soul. Our national story unifies us, strengthens us, and inspires us. This generation will have failed America if we let our national story die with us. We must pass it on.

Yet, in this crucial moment in time, Americans seem to know less and less about the history that has created our identity. A recent study of students at fifty-five leading universities found that more than a third were unable to identify the Constitution as the document that establishes the division of powers in our government.[1] A National Assessment of Education Progress test found that more than half of high school seniors could not identify on which side we fought during World War II.[2]

In a study of college students commissioned by the Intercollegiate Studies Institute (ISI), nearly half of the participants did not know that the Federalist Papers were written in support of ratifying the Constitution. Forty-eight percent believed that the Revolutionary War concluded at the Battle of Gettysburg. Only 34 percent knew that George Washington was an American general at the Battle of Yorktown. While ignorant of their own history, 98 percent could identify rap singer Snoop Doggy Dogg. Another shocking aspect of the study was the finding that at sixteen of the nation's leading universities, including Brown, Georgetown, Yale, Cornell, Berkeley, and Johns Hopkins, seniors knew less than freshman about American history, foreign affairs, and government.[3]

These recent reports, which reflect that we as a people don't fully understand who we are and where we came from, should evoke at least an equal determination to act. We must do more than build a beautiful memorial to Thomas Jefferson in the nation's capital. We must heed his words: "If a nation expects to be ignorant and free . . . it expects what never was and never will be."

We must renew our determination to pass on our national story to the next generation. According to College Board, the United States was the world's leader in producing college students with bachelor degrees—an indicator of long-term strength. However, today, we rank 12th—in the key age range of 24-34—behind nations like Russia and South Korea in graduating students.[4] Only a tiny handful of research and study programs at American universities focus on the ideas and events that helped to produce the U.S. Constitution. One of these was recently created on the campus of the University of Oklahoma—a new Institute for the American Constitutional Heritage. We need many more like it.

The Institute has done much to increase knowledge of our constitution among our students. It works through publications, guest speakers and special student groups which meet regularly outside of the classroom to discuss our constitution and its history. We also sponsor, each spring, a special campus wide day long "Teach In" for students, faculty, staff, alumnae and state leaders to study a period of American history. Attendees hear leading historians from around the world lecture on the period chosen for the year. So far we have focused on the period of the Revolution and the Ratification of the Constitution, the Civil War, and the period of the Depression and World War II.

Recently, historians like Gordon Wood, David McCullough and Doris Kearns Goodwin have written masterful books which have caused larger numbers of Americans to focus on the people and conditions that led to the creation of the United States as an independent nation. The understanding of our history needs to be as broad as possible. American literature and the creative arts must be included. They hold up a mirror to our society, enabling us to better understand what Americans have experienced in the past.

Ever since I left the Senate, I have been involved in public higher education. There is an increasing emphasis on vocational, professional and specialized courses aimed at producing direct economic benefit. No one disputes the need to teach math, science, and technology. According to the Organization for Economic Cooperation and Development, American students rank 25th in math and 21st in science compared to students in 30 industrialized countries. We must regain our competitive edge academically to compete economically. However, presidents, chancellors, and boards of regents must have the courage to insist that teaching courses in the humanities will not be sacrificed. We must make sure that changes in curriculum or in the allocation of recourses do not come at the expense of teaching about our own history and culture.

If we learn nothing of our own history, literature, and creative arts, we will become what someone has called "a nation of skilled barbarians." We should begin by examining the curriculum at K–12 schools and improve it. College and university graduation requirements must be changed to include the study of American history and government at the college level in order to graduate. Today less than 10 percent of American colleges require it.

For a long time, I have called attention to the need for American education to do more to encourage the study of other cultures and to promote study abroad at The University of Oklahoma. It is imperative that we increase our understanding of the rest of the world. However, we must not trade off the study of American history and government in order to do so. We have sidestepped the obvious need for core requirements essential to civic literacy, because we do not want to set off controversies about what we should require all students to study. We can no longer allow a timid political correctness to paralyze us. We must take action.

Justin Dyer has provided a valuable resource to help us combat this civic apathy and stem the tide in our declining civic literacy. *American Soul: The Contested Legacy of the Declaration of Independence* is an essential collection of historical documents that examines the fascinating history of our Declaration of Independence and allows us to take steps toward meeting our duty to learn about how our nation became great.

Introduction

Writing from Philadelphia in the summer of 1776, John Adams predicted in a letter to his wife Abigail that the second day of July would "be the most memorable Epocha, in the History of America."[1] The revolutionary leader envisioned a national holiday celebrating the adoption of a congressional resolution proclaiming that the "United Colonies are, and of right ought to be, free and independent states."[2] That resolution, written by Richard Henry Lee, was, in fact, the nation's first declaration of independence from the British Crown. Yet the day that lives on in the American memory is not the second, but the fourth, of July, and the document remembered as our first national act is not Lee's resolution but Thomas Jefferson's declaration of the causes and justifications for our separation.

The purpose of Jefferson's declaration was to offer reasons for an independence already proclaimed, and the reasons for the act, perhaps more than the act itself, have become part of our national identity. America, as it has often been noted, is unique in its founding commitment to a political creed. That creed, set forth in the Declaration of Independence, reflects a general set of ideas that held sway over many of the men who were instrumental in forging the American Revolution, and, though contested, those ideas have ever been a mainstay of American political culture. "We hold these truths to be self-evident," the familiar words of the Declaration insist, "that all men are created equal, that they are endowed by their Creator with certain unalienable Rights, that among these are Life, Liberty, and the Pursuit of Happiness." In the Declaration the presentation of these principles has all of the qualities of dogma. It is not so much an argument as an assertion. God created men equal in dignity and rights. Governments exist to secure these rights. And when rulers fail in this sacred trust it is the right—even duty—of the people to throw off the chains of tyranny.

And yet, as English journalist and cultural critic G. K. Chesterton noted in the early twentieth century, the general disposition of modern men has been to "say something more like this: 'We hold these truths to be probable enough for pragmatists; that all things looking like men were evolved somehow, being endowed by heredity and environment with no equal rights, but very unequal wrongs,' and so on."[3] While not following this script exactly, a prominent American historian—writing the same year as Chesterton—did suggest something quite similar. "To ask whether the natural rights philosophy in the Declaration is true or false," Professor Carl Becker wrote in his seminal intellectual history of the Declaration, "is essentially a meaningless question."[4] Chesterton, however, thought that democracy had no basis "except in a dogma about the divine origin of man,"[5] and it was dangerous, he presciently warned, to tinker with this dogma by treating notions of natural rights and man's place within a divinely constituted cosmos as essentially meaningless. "Men will more and more realize that there is no meaning in democracy," he suggested, "if there is no meaning in anything; and there is no meaning in anything if the universe has not a centre of significance and an authority that is the author of our rights."[6]

Before his death at the close of World War II, Becker, as well, acknowledged that the "incredible cynicism and brutality of Adolf Hitler's ambitions" had "forced men everywhere to re-appraise the validity of half-forgotten ideas, and enabled them once more to entertain convictions as to the substance of things not evident to the senses."[7] Against the backdrop of modern totalitarianism, there was something persistent and enduring about the Declaration. It spoke to the permanent, immaterial things in human existence—sovereignty, justice, liberty, equality, dignity, and orders both human and divine. And against the atrocities and human rights abuses of the twentieth century, it seemed inadequate to describe the natural rights philosophy of the Declaration as merely a quaint or idiosyncratic relic of a bygone era.

Still, the legacy of those political ideas has been contested throughout the country's short history, and the principles laid out in the first two paragraphs of the Declaration have been the focal point for an enduring public debate about the meaning and purpose of the American experiment. The present volume brings together in one place a variety of interpretations of the Declaration (and, by extension, America) by politicians and statesmen from John Adams and Thomas Jefferson to George W. Bush and Barack Obama. It begins with several early Fourth of July orations, moving through the antislavery movement to Reconstruction, the Progressive Era, the New Deal, the modern civil rights movement, and, finally, the speeches and writings of our most recent presidents.

In any such volume, Abraham Lincoln must occupy a unique place, for it was Lincoln, perhaps more than any other American statesman, who made the Declaration the centerpiece of his political rhetoric. "All this is not the result of accident," the sixteenth president observed as he considered America's growth and success in the nineteenth century. "Without the *Constitution* and the *Union*, we could not have attained the result; but even these are not the primary cause of our great prosperity." The cause of American greatness, Lincoln went on to declare, was the principle of "liberty to all" set forth in our founding document, and, alluding to an ancient Hebrew proverb, Lincoln gave his own interpretation of the central place of the Declaration in American politics:

> The assertion of that *principle*, at *that time*, was *the* word, "fitly spoken" which has proved an "apple of gold" to us. The *Union*, and the *Constitution*, are the *picture* of *silver*, subsequently framed around it. The picture was made, not to *conceal* or *destroy* the apple: but to *adorn* and *preserve* it. The *picture* was made *for* the apple—*not* the apple for the picture.
>
> So let us act, that neither *picture*, or *apple* shall ever be blurred, or bruised, or broken.
>
> That we may so act, we must study, and understand the points of danger.[8]

The immediate points of danger for Lincoln were bound up with Chief Justice Roger B. Taney's notorious opinion in *Dred Scott* v. *Sandford* (1857), which asserted, in part, that African slaves and their descendants were not meant to share in the natural rights appealed to in the Declaration of Independence and that the right to own slaves was "distinctly and expressly affirmed in the Constitution."

In his celebrated debates with Illinois Senator Stephen Douglas, Lincoln later maintained, in contrast, that whoever "teaches that the negro has no share, humble though it may be, in the Declaration of Independence, is going back to the era of our liberty and independence, and, so far as in him lies, muzzling the cannon that thunders its annual joyous return [on the Fourth of July] . . . [while] blowing out the moral lights around us."[9] Five years after his debates with Douglas, Lincoln went so far as to identify the birth of the nation itself with the events of 1776. "Four score and seven years ago," the President declared at the dedication of a national war cemetery at Gettysburg, Pennsylvania, "our fathers brought forth on this continent, a new nation, conceived in Liberty, and dedicated to the proposition that all men are created equal."[10]

In a stinging historical rebuke to Taney's interpretation of the Declaration, Martin Luther King Jr. then stood atop the steps of the Lincoln Memorial, a century after the Gettysburg Address, and appealed to the immortal words of the Declaration. "In a sense we've come to the nation's capital to cash a check," the civil rights leader explained.

When the architects of our republic wrote the magnificent words of the Declaration of Independence, they were signing a promissory note to which every American was to fall heir. This note was a promise that all men, yes black men as well as white men, would be guaranteed the "unalienable rights" of "Life, Liberty, and the Pursuit of Happiness."[11]

Less than fifty years later, Senator Barack Obama—who would soon be the first black American elected to the nation's highest office—delivered a speech at the Constitution Center in Philadelphia in which he argued that the original Constitution, interpreted in light of the principles announced in the Declaration, "had at its very core the ideal of equal citizenship under the law."[12] Yet, as monumental as these developments are, racial egalitarianism is not the only cause that has enlisted the Declaration in its own service. It is, in fact, a document with a meaning and legacy that are continually being contested and shaped. From economic and cultural issues to the contemporary debates about American foreign policy—the Declaration is today, as it has been, a vibrant and dynamic, though perennially disputed, source of American ideals.

Assembled together, the documents in this volume paint, with broad strokes, the contours of the debates over the meaning and legacy of the Declaration of Independence. Part I focuses on the formative years of the American Republic, capped by the deaths of John Adams and Thomas Jefferson on the Fourth of July 1826. Part II centers on the tension between the principles in the Declaration and the institution of slavery, which was central to American political and constitutional development in the nineteenth century. Part III then looks at the Declaration's legacy in the modern world, culling representative speeches and documents pertaining to topics as varied as women's suffrage, progressivism, the civil rights movement, and contemporary economic and foreign policy. While the documents are accompanied by brief historical headnotes, they are deliberately left without commentary and with only minimal editing so that the reader will be able to interact directly with the arguments of some of the most influential interpreters of the Declaration. Indeed, this project had its genesis in a conviction that it is an important and worthwhile endeavor for every citizen to reflect on the contested meaning and legacy of America's founding document.

# I
THE DECLARATION AND THE AMERICAN FOUNDING

1

The Declaration of Independence

Continental Congress, 1776

On June 7, 1776, Richard Henry Lee introduced a resolution to the Continental Congress declaring, "these United Colonies are, and of right ought to be, free and independent States." Lee's resolution was approved by Congress on July 2, 1776. The document that has come to be known as the Declaration of Independence was, however, approved two days later, on July 4, and its main purpose was to offer reasons and justifications for independence.

THE UNANIMOUS DECLARATION OF THE THIRTEEN UNITED STATES OF AMERICA IN CONGRESS, JULY 4, 1776.

WHEN, in the Course of human Events, it becomes necessary for one People to dissolve the Political Bands which have connected them with another, and to assume, among the Powers of the Earth, the separate and equal Station to which the Laws of Nature and of Nature's GOD entitle them, a decent Respect to the Opinions of Mankind requires that they should declare the Causes which impel them to the Separation.

We hold these Truths to be self-evident, that all Men are created equal, that they are endowed, by their CREATOR, with certain unalienable Rights, that among these are Life, Liberty, and the Pursuit of Happiness.— That to secure these Rights, Governments are instituted among Men, deriving their just Powers from the Consent of the Governed, that whenever any Form of Government becomes destructive of these Ends, it is the Right of the People to alter or to abolish it, and to institute new Government, laying its Foundation on such Principles, and organizing its Powers in such Form, as to them shall seem most likely to effect their Safety and Happiness. Prudence, indeed, will dictate, that Governments long established, should not be changed for light and transient Causes; and accordingly all Experience hath shewn, that Mankind are more disposed to suffer, while Evils are sufferable, than to right themselves by abolishing the Forms to which they are accustomed. But when a long Train of Abuses and Usurpations, pursuing invariably the same Object, evinces a Design to reduce them under absolute Despotism, it is their Right, it is their Duty, to throw off such Government, and to provide new Guards for their future Security. Such has been the patient Sufferance of these Colonies; and such is now the Necessity which constrains them to alter their former Systems of Government. The History of the present King of Great-Britain is a History of repeated Injuries and Usurpations, all having in direct Object the Establishment of an absolute Tyranny over these States. To prove this, let Facts be submitted to a candid World.

HE has refused his Assent to Laws, the most wholesome and necessary for the public Good.

HE has forbidden his Governors to pass Laws of immediate and pressing Importance, unless suspended in their Operation till his Assent should be obtained; and when so suspended, he has utterly neglected to attend to them.

HE has refused to pass other Laws for the Accommodation of large Districts of People, unless those People would relinquish the Right of Representation in the Legislature, a Right inestimable to them, and formidable to Tyranny only.

HE has called together Legislative Bodies at Places unusual, uncomfortable, and distant from the Depository of their public Records, for the sole Purpose of fatiguing them into Compliance with his Measures.

HE has dissolved Representative Houses repeatedly, for opposing with manly Firmness his Invasions on the Rights of the People.

HE has refused for a long Time, after such Dissolutions, to cause others to be elected; whereby the Legislative Powers, incapable of Annihilation, have returned to the People at large for their exercise; the State remaining, in the mean Time, exposed to all the Dangers of Invasion from without, and Convulsions within.

HE has endeavoured to prevent the Population of these States; for that Purpose obstructing the Laws for Naturalization of Foreigners; refusing to pass others to encourage their Migrations hither, and raising the Conditions of new Appropriations of Lands.

HE has obstructed the Administration of Justice, by refusing his Assent to Laws for establishing Judiciary Powers.

HE has made Judges dependent on his Will alone, for the Tenure of their Offices, and the Amount and Payment of their Salaries.

HE has erected a Multitude of new Offices, and sent hither Swarms of Officers to harrass our People, and eat out their Substance.

HE has kept among us, in Times of Peace, Standing Armies, without the Consent of our Legislatures.

HE has affected to render the Military independent of and superior to the Civil Power.

HE has combined with others to subject us to a Jurisdiction foreign to our Constitution, and unacknowledged by our Laws; giving his Assent to their Acts of pretended Legislation:

FOR quartering large Bodies of Armed Troops among us:

FOR protecting them, by a mock Trial, from Punishment for any Murders which they should commit on the Inhabitants of these States:

FOR cutting off our Trade with all Parts of the World:

FOR imposing Taxes on us without our Consent:

FOR depriving us, in many Cases, of the Benefits of Trial by Jury:

FOR transporting us beyond Seas to be tried for pretended Offences:

FOR abolishing the free System of English Laws in a neighbouring Province, establishing therein an arbitrary Government, and enlarging its Boundaries, so as to render it at once an Example and fit Instrument for introducing the same absolute Rule into these Colonies:

FOR taking away our Charters, abolishing our most valuable Laws, and altering fundamentally the Forms of our Governments:

FOR suspending our own Legislatures, and declaring themselves invested with Power to legislate for us in all Cases whatsoever.

HE has abdicated Government here, by declaring us out of his Protection, and waging War against us.

HE has plundered our Seas, ravaged our Coasts, burnt our Towns, and destroyed the Lives of our People.

HE is, at this Time, transporting large Armies of foreign Mercenaries to complete the Works of Death, Desolation, and Tyranny, already begun with Circumstances of Cruelty and Perfidy, scarcely paralleled in the most barbarous Ages, and totally unworthy the Head of a civilized Nation.

HE has constrained our Fellow-Citizens, taken Captive on the high Seas, to bear Arms against their Country, to become the Executioners of their Friends and Brethren, or to fall themselves by their Hands.

HE has excited domestic Insurrections amongst us, and has endeavoured to bring on the Inhabitants of our Frontiers, the merciless Indian Savages, whose known Rule of Warfare, is an undistinguished Destruction, of all Ages, Sexes, and Conditions.

IN every Stage of these Oppressions we have Petitioned for Redress in the most humble Terms: Our repeated Petitions have been answered only by repeated Injury. A Prince, whose Character is thus marked by every Act which may define a Tyrant, is unfit to be the Ruler of a free People.

NOR have we been wanting in Attentions to our British Brethren. We have warned them, from Time to Time, of Attempts by their Legislature to extend an unwarrantable Jurisdiction over us. We have reminded them of the Circumstances of our Emigration and Settlement here. We have appealed to their native Justice and Magnanimity, and we have conjured them by the Ties of our common Kindred to disavow these Usurpations, which would inevitably interrupt our Connexions and Correspondence. They too have been deaf to the Voice of Justice and of Consanguinity. We must, therefore, acquiesce in the Necessity, which denounces our Separation, and hold them, as we hold the Rest of Mankind, Enemies in War, in Peace Friends.

WE, therefore, the Representatives of the UNITED STATES OF AMERICA, in GENERAL CONGRESS Assembled, appealing to the Supreme Judge of the World for the Rectitude of our Intentions, do, in the Name, and by Authority of the good People of these Colonies, solemnly Publish and Declare, That these United Colonies are, and of Right ought to be, FREE AND INDEPENDENT STATES; that they are absolved from all Allegiance to the British Crown, and that all political Connexion between them and the State of Great-Britain, is, and ought to be, totally dissolved; and that as FREE AND INDEPENDENT STATES, they have full Power to levy War, conclude Peace, contract Alliances, establish Commerce, and to do all other Acts and Things which INDEPENDENT STATES may of Right do. And for the Support of this Declaration, with a firm Reliance on the Protection of DIVINE PROVIDENCE, we mutually pledge to each other our Lives, our Fortunes, and our sacred Honour.

2

Rough Draft of the Declaration of Independence

Thomas Jefferson, 1776

> *This is a reconstruction of Thomas Jefferson's original "rough draft" of the Declaration of Independence. A committee composed of Thomas Jefferson (1743–1826), John Adams (1735–1826), Benjamin Franklin (1706–1790), Roger Sherman (1721–1793), and Robert Livingston (1746–1813) was tasked with drafting a Declaration of Independence, and the committee, Jefferson later reported, "desired me to do it." The bold and underlined portions are the parts of Jefferson's original draft that were eventually removed by Congress; bold and bracketed portions are additions made by Congress to the original draft.*

<u>A Declaration of the Representatives of the UNITED STATES OF AMERICA, in General Congress assembled.</u> [The unanimous declaration of the thirteen United States of America in Congress, July 4, 1776]
When in the course of human events it becomes necessary for **<u>a</u>** [one] people to **<u>advance from that subordination in which they have hitherto remained</u>** [dissolve the Political Bands which have connected them with another], & to assume among the powers of the earth the **<u>equal & independant</u>** [separate and equal] station to which the laws of nature & of nature's god entitle them, a decent respect to the opinions of mankind requires that they should declare the causes which impel them to the **<u>change</u>** [separation].
We hold these truths to be **<u>sacred & undeniable</u>** [self-evident]; that all men are created equal **<u>& independant</u>**, that **<u>from that equal creation they derive rights inherent & inalienable among which are the preservation of</u>** [they are endowed, by their CREATOR, with certain inalienable rights, that among these are] life, & liberty, & the pursuit of happiness; that to secure these **<u>ends</u>** [rights], governments are instituted

among men, deriving their just powers from the consent of the governed; that whenever any form of government shall become destructive of these ends, it is the right of the people to alter or to abolish it, & to institute new government, laying it's foundation on such principles & organising it's powers in such form, as to them shall seem most likely to effect their safety & happiness. prudence indeed will dictate that governments long established should not be changed for light & transient causes: and accordingly all experience hath shewn that mankind are more disposed to suffer while evils are sufferable, than to right themselves by abolishing the forms to which they are accustomed. but when a long train of abuses & usurpations, **begun at a distinguished period, &** pursuing invariably the same object, evinces a design to **subject** [reduce] them **to arbitrary power** [under absolute despotism] it is their right, it is their duty, to throw off such government & to provide new guards for their future security. such has been the patient sufferance of these colonies; & such is now the necessity which constrains them to alter their former systems of government. the history of his present **majesty** [King of Great-Britain], is a history of **unremitting** [repeated] injuries and usurpations, **among which no one fact stands single or solitary to contradict the uniform tenor of the rest**, all **of which have** [having] in direct object the establishment of an absolute tyranny over these states. to prove this, let facts be submitted to a candid world[.]**, for the truth of which we pledge a faith yet unsullied by falsehood.** HE has refused his assent to laws the most wholesome and necessary for the public good:

HE has forbidden his governors to pass laws of immediate & pressing importance, unless suspended in their operation till his assent should be obtained; and when so suspended, he has neglected utterly to attend to them.

HE has refused to pass other laws for the accomodation of large districts of people unless those people would relinquish the right of representation [in the legislature], a right inestimable to them, & formidable to tyrants **alone** [only]:

[**HE has called together Legislative Bodies at Places unusual, uncomfortable, and distant from the Depository of their public Records, for the sole Purpose of fatiguing them into Compliance with his Measures.**]

HE has dissolved Representative houses repeatedly **& continually**, for opposing with manly firmness his invasions on the rights of the people:

HE has refused for a long **space of** time, [after such Dissolutions,] to cause others to be elected, whereby the legislative powers, incapable of annihilation, have returned to the people at large for their exercise, the state remaining in the mean time exposed to all the dangers of invasion from without, & convulsions within:

HE has endeavored to prevent the population of these states; for that purpose obstructing the laws for naturalization of foreigners; refusing to pass others to encourage their migrations hither; & raising the conditions of new appropriations of lands:

HE has **suffered** [obstructed] the administration of justice **totally to cease in some of these colonies,** [by] refusing his assent to laws for establishing judiciary powers:

HE has made our judges dependant on his will alone, for the tenure of their offices, and [the] amount of their salaries:

HE has erected a multitude of new offices **by a self-assumed power,** & sent hither swarms of [new] officers to harrass our people & eat out their substance:

HE has kept among us in times of peace standing armies **& ships of war:** [without the Consent of our Legislatures]

HE has affected to render the military, independant of & superior to the civil power:

HE has combined with others to subject us to a jurisdiction foreign to our **constitutions** [Constitution] and unacknowledged by our laws; giving his assent to their pretended acts of legislation;

FOR quartering large bodies of armed troops among us;

FOR protecting them by a mock-trial from punishment for any murders [which] they should commit on the inhabitants of these states;

FOR cutting off our trade with all parts of the world;

FOR imposing taxes on us without our consent;

FOR depriving us [, **in many cases,**] of the benefits of trial by jury;

FOR transporting us beyond seas to be tried for pretended offences:

[**FOR abolishing the free System of English Laws in a neighbouring Province, establishing therein an arbitrary Government, and enlarging its Boundaries, so as to render it at once an Example and fit Instrument for introducing the same absolute Rule into these Colonies:**]

FOR taking away our charters, [**abolishing our most valuable Laws**] & altering fundamentally the forms of our governments;

FOR suspending our own legislatures & declaring themselves invested with power to legislate for us in all cases whatsoever:

HE has abdicated government here, [**by declaring us out of his Protection, and waging War against us**] withdrawing his governors, & declaring us out of his allegiance & protection:

HE has plundered our seas, ravaged our coasts, burnt our towns & destroyed the lives of our people:

HE is at this time transporting large armies of foreign mercenaries to compleat the works of death, desolation & tyranny, already begun with circumstances of cruelty & perfidy [scarcely paralleled in the most barbarous Ages, and totally] unworthy the head of a civilized nation:

[**HE has constrained our Fellow-Citizens, taken Captive on the high seas, to bear Arms against their Country, to become the Executioners of their Friends and Brethren, or to fall themselves by their Hands.**]

HE has [excited domestic Insurrections amongst us, and has] endeavored to bring on the inhabitants of our frontiers the merciless Indian savages, whose known rule of warfare is an undistinguished destruction of all ages, sexes, & conditions **of existence:**

HE has incited treasonable insurrections in our fellow-subjects, with the allurements of forfeiture & confiscation of our property:

HE has waged cruel war against human nature itself, violating it's most sacred rights of life & liberty in the persons of a distant people who never offended him, captivating & carrying them into slavery in another hemisphere, or to incur miserable death in their transportation thither. this piratical warfare, the opprobrium of *infidel* powers, is the warfare of the CHRISTIAN king of Great Britain. determined to keep open a market where MEN should be bought & sold, he has prostituted his negative for suppressing every legislative attempt to prohibit or to restrain this execrable commerce: and that this assemblage of horrors might want no fact of distinguished die, he is now exciting those very people to rise in arms among us, and to purchase that liberty of which *he* has deprived them, by murdering the people upon whom *he* also obtruded them; thus paying off former crimes committed against the *liberties* of one people, with crimes which he urges them to commit against the *lives* of another.

IN every stage of these oppressions we have petitioned for redress in the most humble terms; our repeated petitions have been answered by repeated injury. a prince whose character is thus marked by every act which may define a tyrant, is unfit to be the ruler of a [free] people[.] **who mean to be free. future ages will scarce believe that the hardiness of one man, adventured within the short compass of 12 years only, on so many acts of tyranny without a mask, over a people fostered & fixed in principles of liberty**

NOR have we been wanting in attentions to our British brethren. we have warned them from time to time of attempts by their legislature to extend a jurisdiction over **these our states** [us]. we have reminded them of the circumstances of our emigration & settlement here, **no one of which could warrant so strange a pretension: that these were effected at the expence of our own blood & treasure, unassisted by the wealth or the strength of Great Britain: that in constituting indeed our several forms of government, we had adopted one common king, thereby laying a foundation for perpetual league & amity with them: but that submission to their parliament was no part of our constitution, nor ever in idea, if history may be credited: and** we [have] appealed to their native justice & magnanimity, **as well as** [and we have conjured them] to the ties of our common kindred to disavow these usurpations which **were likely to** [would inevitably] interrupt our **correspondence & connection** [Connexions and Correspondence]. they too have been deaf to the voice of justice & of consanguinity, **& when occasions have been given them, by the regular** course of their laws, of removing from their councils the disturbers of our harmony, they have by their free election re-established them in power. at this very time too they are permitting their chief magistrate to send over not only soldiers of our common blood, but Scotch & foreign mercenaries to invade & deluge us in blood. these facts have given the last stab to agonizing affection, and manly spirit bids us to renounce for ever these unfeeling brethren. we must [therefore, acquiesce in the Necessity, which denounces our Separation and] endeavor to forget our former love for them, and to hold them as we hold the rest of mankind, enemies in war, in peace friends. we might have been a free & a great people together; but a communication of grandeur & of freedom it seems is below their dignity. be it so, since they will have it: the road to glory & happiness is open to us too; we will climb it in a separate state, and acquiesce in the necessity which pronounces our everlasting Adieu!

WE therefore the representatives of the United States of America in General Congress assembled, [appealing to the Supreme Judge of the World for the Rectitude of our Intentions] do, in the name & by authority of the good people of these **states** [colonies], [solemnly Publish and Declare] reject and renounce all allegiance & subjection to the kings of Great Britain & all others who may hereafter claim by, through, or under them; we utterly dissolve & break off all political connection which may have heretofore subsisted between us & the people or parliament of Great Britain; and finally we do assert and declare [that] these [United] colonies [are, and of Right ought] to be free and independant states, and that as free & independant states they shall hereafter [that they] have [full] power to levy war, conclude peace, contract alliances, establish commerce, & to do all other acts and things which independant states may of right do. And for the support of this declaration, [with a firm Reliance on the Protection of DIVINE PROVIDENCE], we mutually pledge to each other our lives, our fortunes, & our sacred honour.

3

Letters to Abigail

John Adams, 1776

John Adams (1735–1826) was a member of the committee in charge of drafting a declaration of independence, and he penned the following letters to his wife, Abigail, on July 3, 1776.

—Philadelphia July 3, 1776

Your Favour of June 17 dated at Plymouth, was handed me, by yesterdays Post. I was much pleased to find that you had taken a journey to Plymouth, to see your Friends in the long Absence of one whom you may wish to see. The Excursion will be an Amusement, and will serve your Health. How happy would it have made me to have taken this journey with you?

I was informed, a day or two before the Receipt of your Letter, that you were gone to Plymouth, by Mrs. Polly Palmer, who was obliging enough in your Absence, to inform me, of the Particulars of the Expedition to the lower Harbour against the Men of War. Her Narration is executed, with a Precision and Perspicuity, which would have become the Pen of an accomplished Historian.

I am very glad you had so good an opportunity of seeing one of our little American Men of War. Many Ideas, new to you, must have presented themselves in such a Scene; and you will in future, better understand the Relations of Sea Engagements.

I rejoice extreamly at Dr. Bulfinches Petition to open an Hospital. But I hope, the Business will be done upon a larger Scale. I hope, that one Hospital will be licensed in every County, if not in every Town. I am happy to find you resolved, to be with the Children, in the first Class.

Mr. Whitney and Mrs. Katy Quincy, are cleverly through Innoculation, in this City.

I have one favour to ask, and that is, that in your future Letters, you would acknowledge the Receipt of all those you may receive from me, and mention their Dates. By this Means I shall know if any of mine miscarry.

The Information you give me of our Friends refusing his Appointment, has given me much Pain, Grief and Anxiety. I believe I shall be obliged to follow his Example. I have not Fortune enough to support my Family, and what is of more Importance, to support the Dignity of that exalted Station.

It is too high and lifted up, for me; who delight in nothing so much as Retreat, Solitude, Silence, and Obscurity. In private Life, no one has a Right to censure me for following my own Inclinations, in Retirement, Simplicity, and Frugality: in public Life, every Man has a Right to remark as he pleases, at least he thinks so.

Yesterday the greatest Question was decided, which ever was debated in America, and a greater perhaps, never was or will be decided among Men. A Resolution was passed without one dissenting Colony "that these united Colonies, are, and of right ought to be free and independent States, and as such, they have, and of Right ought to have full Power to make War, conclude Peace, establish Commerce, and to do all the other Acts and Things, which other States may rightfully do." You will see in a few days a Declaration setting forth the Causes, which have impell'd Us to this mighty Revolution, and the Reasons which will justify it, in the Sight of God and Man. A Plan of Confederation will be taken up in a few days.

When I look back to the Year 1761, and recollect the Argument concerning Writs of Assistance, in the Superiour Court, which I have hitherto considered as the Commencement of the Controversy, between Great Britain and America, and run through the whole Period from that Time to this, and recollect the series of political Events, the Chain of Causes and Effects, I am surprized at the Suddenness, as well as Greatness of this Revolution. Britain has been fill'd with Folly, and America with Wisdom, at least this is my judgment. —Time must determine. It is the Will of Heaven, that the two Countries should be sundered forever. It may be the Will of Heaven that America shall suffer Calamities still more wasting and Distresses yet more dreadfull. If this is to be the Case, it will have this good Effect, at least: it will inspire Us with many Virtues, which We have not, and correct many Errors, Follies, and Vices, which threaten to disturb, dishonour, and destroy Us. —The Furnace of Affliction produces Refinement, in States as well as Individuals. And the new Governments we are assuming, in every Part, will require a Purification from our Vices, and an Augmentation of our Virtues or they will be no Blessings. The People will have unbounded Power. And the People are extreamly addicted to Corruption and Venality, as well as the Great. —But I must submit all my Hopes and Fears, to an overruling Providence, in which, unfashionable [as] the Faith may be, I firmly believe.

Philadelphia July 3d. 1776

Had a Declaration of Independency been made seven Months ago, it would have been attended with many great and glorious Effects. . . . We might before this Hour, have formed Alliances with foreign States. —We should have mastered Quebec and been in Possession of Canada. . . . You will perhaps wonder, how such a Declaration would have influenced our Affairs, in Canada, but if I could write with Freedom I could easily convince you, that it would, and explain to you the manner how. —Many Gentlemen in high Stations and of great Influence have been duped, by the ministerial Bubble of Commissioners to treat. . . . And in real, sincere Expectation of this Event, which they so fondly wished, they have been slow and languid, in promoting Measures for the Reduction of that Province. Others there are in the Colonies who really wished that our Enterprise in Canada would be defeated, that the Colonies might be brought into Danger and Distress between two Fires, and be thus induced to submit. Others really wished to defeat the Expedition to Canada, lest the Conquest of it, should elevate the Minds of the People too much to hearken to those Terms of Reconciliation which they believed would be offered Us. These jarring Views, Wishes and Designs, occasioned an opposition to many salutary Measures, which were proposed for the Support of that Expedition, and caused Obstructions, Embarrassments and studied Delays, which have finally, lost Us the Province.

All these Causes however in Conjunction would not have disappointed Us, if it had not been for a Misfortune, which could not be foreseen, and perhaps could not have been prevented, I mean the Prevalence of the small Pox among our Troops. . . . This fatal Pestilence compleated our Destruction. —It is a Frown of Providence upon Us, which We ought to lay to heart.

But on the other Hand, the Delay of this Declaration to this Time, has many great Advantages attending it. —The Hopes of Reconciliation, which were fondly entertained by Multitudes of honest and well meaning tho weak and mistaken People, have been gradually and at last totally extinguished. —Time has been given for the whole People, maturely to consider the great Question of Independence and to ripen their judgments, dissipate their Fears, and allure their Hopes, by discussing it in News Papers and Pamphletts, by debating it, in Assemblies, Conventions, Committees of Safety and Inspection, in Town and County Meetings, as well as in private Conversations, so that the whole People in every Colony of the 13, have now adopted it, as their own Act. -- This will cement the Union, and avoid those Heats and perhaps Convulsions which might have been occasioned, by such a Declaration Six Months ago.

But the Day is past. The Second Day of July 1776, will be the most memorable Epocha, in the History of America.

I am apt to believe that it will be celebrated, by succeeding Generations, as the great anniversary Festival. It ought to be commemorated, as the Day of Deliverance by solemn Acts of Devotion to God Almighty. It ought to be solemnized with Pomp and Parade, with Shews Games, Sports, Guns, Bells, Bonfires and Illuminations from one End of this Continent to the other from this Time forward forever more.

You will think me transported with Enthusiasm but I am not. —I am well aware of the Toil and Blood and Treasure, that it will cost Us to maintain this Declaration, and support and defend these States. —Yet through all the Gloom I can see the Rays of ravishing Light and Glory. I can see that the End is more than worth all the Means. And that Posterity will tryumph in that Days Transaction, even altho We should rue it, which I trust in God We shall not.

4

A Short Review of the Declaration

Jeremy Bentham, 1776

> *When a copy of the Declaration reached England, the government commissioned a response by conservative pamphleteer John Lind (1737–1781) and philosopher Jeremy Bentham (1748–1832). Most of their work was a point-by-point rebuttal to the charges leveled against the King. In his "Short Review of the Declaration," however, Bentham took particular aim at the "theory of Government" put forward in the preamble to the Declaration.*

In examining this singular Declaration, I have hitherto confined myself to what are given as *facts*, and alleged against his Majesty and his Parliament, in support of the charge of tyranny and usurpation. Of the preamble I have taken little or no notice. The truth is, little or none does it deserve. The opinions of the modern Americans on Government, like those of their good ancestors on witchcraft, would be too ridiculous to deserve any notice, if like them too, contemptible and extravagant as they be, they had not led to the most serious evils.

In this preamble however it is, that they attempt to establish a *theory of Government*; a theory, as absurd and visionary, as the system of conduct in defence of which it is established, is nefarious. Here it is, that maxims are advanced in justification of their enterprise against the British Government. To these maxims, adduced for *this purpose*, it would be sufficient to say, that they are *repugnant to the British Constitution*. But beyond this they are subversive of every actual or imaginable kind of Government.

They are about *"to assume,"* as they tell us, *"among the powers of the earth, that equal and separate station to which"*—they have lately discovered—*"the laws of Nature, and of Nature's God entitle them."* What difference these acute legislators suppose between the *laws of Nature, and of Nature's God*, is more than I can take upon me to determine, or even to guess. If to what they now demand they were entitled by any law of God, they had only to produce that law, and all controversy was at an end. Instead of this, what do they produce? What they call self-evident truths. "*All men,*" they tell us, "are created equal." This surely is a new discovery; now, for the first time, we learn, that a child, at the moment of his birth, has the same quantity of *natural* power as the parent, the same quantity of *political* power as the magistrate.

The rights of "*life, liberty, and the pursuit of happiness*"—by which, if they mean any thing, they must mean the right to *enjoy* life, to *enjoy* liberty, and the *pursue* happiness—they "hold to be inalienable." This they "hold to be among *truths self-evident.*" At the same time, to secure these rights, they are content that Governments should be instituted. They perceive not, or will not seem to perceive, that nothing which can be called Government ever was, or ever could be, in any instance, exercised, but at the expence of one or other of those rights.—That, consequently, in as many instances as Government is ever exercised, some one or other of these rights, pretended to be unalienable, is actually alienated.

That men are engaged in the design of subverting a lawful Government, should endeavour by a cloud of words, to throw a veil over their design; that they should endeavour to beat down the criteria between tyranny and lawful government, is not at all surprising. But rather surprising it must certainly appear, that they should advance maxims so incompatible with their present conduct. If the right of enjoying life be unalienable, whence came their invasion of his Majesty's province of Canada? Whence the unprovoked destruction of so many lives of the inhabitants of that province? If the right of enjoying liberty be unalienable, whence came so many of his Majesty's peaceable subjects among them, without any offence, without so much as a pretended offence, merely for being suspected not to wish well to their enormities, to be held by them in durance? If the right of pursuing happiness be unalienable, how is it that so many others of their fellow-citizens are by the same injustice and violence made miserable, their fortunes ruined, their persons banished and driven from their friends and families? Or would they have it believed, that there is in their selves some superior sanctity, some peculiar privilege, by which those things are lawful to them, which are unlawful to all the world besides? Or is it, that among acts of coercion, acts by which life or liberty are taken away, and the pursuit of happiness restrained, those only are unlawful, which their delinquency has brought upon them, and which are exercised by regular, long established, accustomed governments?

In these tents they have outdone the utmost extravagance of all former fanatics. The German Anabaptists indeed went so far as to speak of the right of enjoying life as a right unalienable. To take away life, even in the Magistrate, they held to be unlawful. But they went no farther, it was reserved for an American Congress, to add to the number of unalienable rights, that of enjoying liberty, and pursuing happiness;—that is,—if they mean any thing,—pursuing it wherever a man thinks he can see it, and by whatever means he thinks he can attain it:—That is, what all *penal* laws—those made by their selves among others—which affect life or liberty, are contrary to the law of God, and the unalienable rights of mankind:—That is, that thieves are not to be restrained from theft, murderers from murder, rebels from rebellion.

Here then they have put the axe to the root of all Government; and yet, in the same breath, they talk of "Government," of Governments "long established," To these last, they attribute some kind of respect; they vouchsafe even to go so far as to admit, that *"Governments, long established, should not be changed for light or transient reasons."*

For what, according to their own shewing, what was their original, their *only original grievance*? That they were actually taxed more than they could bear? No; but that they were *liable* to be taxed. What is the amount of all the subsequent grievances they allege? That they were *actually* oppressed by Government? That Government had actually misused its power? No; but that it was possible they might be oppressed; *possible* that Government might misuse its powers. Is there any where, can there be imagined any where, *that* Government, where subjects are not liable to be taxed more than they can bear? Where it is not possible that subjects may be oppressed, not possible that Government may misuse its powers?

This, I say, is the amount, the *whole sum and substance of all* their grievances. . . . How this Declaration may strike others, I know not. To me, I own, it appears that it cannot fail—to use the words of a great Orator—"of doing us *Knight's* service." The mouth of faction, we may reasonably presume, will be closed; the eyes of those who say not, or would not see, that the Americans were long since aspiring at independence, will be opened; the nation will unite as one man, and teach this rebellious people, that it is one thing for them to *say*, the connection, which bound them to us, is *dissolved*, another to *dissolve* it; that to *accomplish* their *independence* is not quite so easy as to *declare* it: *that there is no peace with them, but with the peace of the King: no war with them, but that war, which offended justice wages against criminals.*—We too, I hope, shall *acquiesce in the necessity* of submitting to whatever burdens, of making whatever efforts may be necessary, to bring this ungrateful and rebellious people back to that allegiance they have long had it in contemplation to renounce, and have now at last so daringly renounced.

5

The American Mind

Thomas Jefferson, 1825

> *In this excerpt from a letter written on the eve of the fiftieth anniversary of the Declaration of Independence, Thomas Jefferson made no pretense to originality but instead described the political ideas in the Declaration as "an expression of the American mind."*

[W]ith respect to our rights, and the acts of the British government contravening those rights, there was but one opinion on this side of the water. All American Whigs thought alike on these subjects. When forced, therefore, to resort to arms for redress, an appeal to the tribunal of the world was deemed proper for our justification. This was the object of the Declaration of Independence. Not to find out new principles, or new arguments, never before thought of, not merely to say things which had never been said before; but to place before mankind the common sense of the subject, in terms so plain and firm as to command their assent, and to justify ourselves in the independent stand we are compelled to take. Neither aiming at originality of principle or sentiment, nor yet copied from any particular and previous writing, it was intended to be an expression of the American mind, and to give to that expression the proper tone and spirit called for by the occasion. All its authority rests then on the harmonizing sentiments of the day, whether expressed in conversation, in letters, printed essays, or in the elementary books of public right, as Aristotle, Cicero, Locke, Sidney, &c. . . .

6

Popular Sovereignty

James Wilson, 1787

> *James Wilson (1742–1798) was both a signer of the Declaration of Independence and a delegate to the constitutional convention in 1787. In his speech at the Pennsylvania ratifying convention, Wilson appealed to the Declaration of Independence in order to argue that the people—rather the state or national governments created by the people— were the "supreme, absolute and uncontrollable" governing authority in America. The debate about the location of sovereignty in the American constitutional order figured prominently in the constitutional conflict that led, ultimately, to the Civil War.*

It has not been, nor, I presume, will it be denied, that somewhere there is, and of necessity must be, a supreme, absolute and uncontrollable authority. This, I believe, may justly be termed the sovereign power; for from that gentleman's (Mr. Findley) account of the matter, it cannot be sovereign, unless it is supreme; for, says he, a subordinate sovereignty is no sovereignty at all. I had the honor of observing, that if the question was asked, where the supreme power resided, different answers would be given by different writers. I mentioned that Blackstone will tell you, that in Britain it is lodged in the British parliament; and I believe there is no writer on this subject on the other side of the Atlantic, but supposes it to be vested in that body. I stated further, that if the question was asked, some politician, who had not considered the subject with sufficient accuracy, where the supreme power resided in our governments, would answer, that it was vested in the State constitutions. This opinion approaches near the truth, but does not reach it; for the truth is, that the supreme, absolute and uncontrollable authority, *remains* with the people. I mentioned also, that the practical recognition of this truth was reserved for the honor of this country. I recollect no constitution founded on this principle: but we have witnessed the improvement, and enjoy the happiness, of seeing it carried into practice. The great and penetrating mind of Locke seems to be the only one that pointed towards even the theory of this great truth.

When I made the observation, that some politicians would say the supreme power was lodged in our State constitutions, I did not suspect that the honorable gentleman from Westmoreland (Mr. Findley) was included in that description; but I find myself disappointed; for I imagined his opposition would arise from another consideration. His position is, that the supreme power resides in the States, as governments; and mine is, that it *resides* in the PEOPLE, as the fountain of government; that the people have not—that the people mean not—and that the people ought not, to part with it to any government whatsoever. In their hands it remains secure. They can delegate it in such proportions, to such bodies, on such terms, and under such limitations, as they think proper. I agree with the members in opposition, that there cannot be two sovereign powers on the same subject.

I consider the people of the United States as forming one great community, and I consider the people of the different States as forming communities again on a lesser scale. From this great division of the people into distinct communities it will be found necessary that different proportions of legislative powers should be given to the governments, according to the nature, number and magnitude of their objects.

Unless the people are considered in these two views, we shall never be able to understand the principle on which this system was constructed. I view the States as made *for* the people as well as *by* them, and not the people as made for the States. The people, therefore, have a right, whilst enjoying the undeniable powers of society, to form either a general government, or state governments, in what manner they please; or to accommodate them to one another, and by this means preserve them all. This, I say, is the inherent and unalienable right of the people, and as an illustration of it, I beg to read a few words from the Declaration of Independence, made by the representatives of the United States, and recognized by the whole Union.— "We hold these truths to be self-evident, that all men are created equal; that they are endowed by their Creator with certain unalienable rights; that among these are life, liberty, and the pursuit of happiness. That to secure these rights, *governments are* instituted among men, *deriving their just powers from the consent of the governed;* that whenever any form of government becomes destructive of these ends, it is the RIGHT of the people to alter or to abolish it, and institute a new government, laying its foundation on such principles, and organizing its powers in such forms, as to them shall seem most likely to effect their safety and happiness."

This is the broad basis on which our independence was placed. On the same certain and solid foundation this system is erected.

7

Keeping the Revolution

Daniel Webster, 1802

Daniel Webster (1782–1852) delivered the following oration on the Fourth of July, 1802, when he was twenty years old. Webster went on to become one of the nineteenth century's most accomplished statesmen, and he is often considered to be among the most talented political orators in American history. Echoing the Declaration's insistence that long established governments ought not be changed "for light and transient causes," Webster devoted the majority of his address to the task of constitutional maintenance in the post-revolutionary era.

In the present situation of our country, it is, my respected fellow-citizens, matter of high joy and congratulation that there is one day in the year on which men of different principles and different opinions can associate together. The Fourth of July is not an occasion to compass sea and land to make proselytes. The good sense and the good nature which yet remain among us will, we trust, prevail on this day, and be sufficient to chain, at least for a season, that untamed monster, Party Spirit—and would to God that it might be chained forever, that, as we have but one interest, we might have but one heart and one mind!

You have hitherto, fellow-citizens, on occasions of this kind, been entertained with the discussion of national questions; with inquiries into the true principles of government; with recapitulations of the War; with speculations on the causes of our Revolution, and on its consequences to ourselves and to the world. Leaving these subjects, it shall be the ambition of the speaker of this day to present such a view of your Constitution and your Union as shall convince you that you have nothing to hope from a change.

This age has been correctly denominated an age of experiments. Innovation is the idol of the times. The human mind seems to have burst its ancient limits, and to be travelling over the face of the material and intellectual creation in search of improvement. The world hath become like a fickle lover, in whom every new face inspires new passion. In this rage for novelty many things are made better, and many things are made worse. Old errors are discarded, and new errors are embraced. Governments feel the same effects from this spirit as every thing else. Some, like our own, grow into beauty and excellence, while others sink still deeper into deformity and wretchedness. The experience of all ages will bear us out in saying, that alterations of political systems are always attended with a greater or lesser degree of danger. They ought, therefore, never to be undertaken, unless the evil complained of be really felt and the prospect of a remedy clearly seen. The politician that undertakes to improve a Constitution with as little thought as a farmer sets about mending his plow, is no master of his trade. If that Constitution be a systematic one, if it be a free one, its parts are so necessarily connected that an alteration in one will work an alteration in all; and this cobbler, however pure and honest his intentions, will, in the end, find that what came to his hands a fair and lovely fabric goes from them a miserable piece of patchwork.

Nor are great and striking alterations alone to be shunned. A succession of small changes, a perpetual tampering with minute parts, steal away the breath though they leave the body; for it is true that a government may lose all its real character, its genius and its temper, without losing its appearance. You may have a despotism under the name of a republic. You may look on a government and see it possess all the external essential modes of freedom, and yet see nothing of the essence, the vitality, of freedom in it: just as you may behold Washington or Franklin in wax-work; the form is perfect, but the spirit, the life, is not there . . .

The American Constitution is the purchase of American valor. It is the rich prize that rewards the toil of eight years of war and of blood: and what is all the pomp of military glory, what are victories, what are armies subdued, fleets captured, colors taken, unless they end in the establishment of wise laws and national happiness? Our Revolution is not more renowned for the brilliancy of its scenes than for the benefit of its consequences. The Constitution is the great memorial of the deeds of our ancestors. On the pillars and on the arches of that dome their names are written and their achievements recorded. While that lasts, while a single page or a single article can be found, it will carry down the record to future ages. It will teach mankind that glory, empty, tinkling glory, was not the object for which Americans fought. Great Britain had carried the fame of her arms far and wide. She had humbled France and Spain; she had reached her arm across the Eastern Continent, and given laws on the banks of the Ganges.

A few scattered colonists did not rise up to contend with such a nation for mere renown. They had a nobler object, and in pursuit of that object they manifested a courage, constancy, and union, that deserve to be celebrated by poets and historians while language lasts.

The valor of America was not a transient, glimmering ray shot forth from the impulse of momentary resentment. Against unjust and arbitrary laws she rose with determined, unalterable spirit. Like the rising sun, clouds and mists hung around her, but her course, like his, brightened as she proceeded. Valor, however, displayed in combat, is a less remarkable trait in the character of our countrymen than the wisdom manifested when the combat was over. All countries and all ages produce warriors, but rare are the instances in which men sit down coolly at the close of their labors to enjoy the fruits of them. Having destroyed one despotism, nations generally create another; having rejected the dominion of one tyrant, they make another for themselves. England beheaded her Charles, but crowned her Cromwell. France guillotined her Louises, but obeys her Bonapartes. Thanks to God, neither foreign nor domestic usurpation flourishes on our soil!

Having thus, fellow-citizens ... paid an inadequate tribute to the wisdom which produced [the Constitution], let us consider seriously its means of preservation. To perpetuate the government we must cherish the love of it. One chief pillar in the republican fabric is the spirit of patriotism ... To preserve the government we must also preserve a correct and energetic tone of morals. After all that can be said, the truth is that liberty consists more in the habits of the people than in anything else. When the public mind becomes vitiated and depraved, every attempt to preserve it is in vain. Laws are a nullity, and a Constitution waste paper. There are always men wicked enough to go any length in the pursuit of power, if they can find others wicked enough to support them. They regard not paper and parchment. Can you stop the progress of a usurper by opposing him the laws of his country? Then you may check the careering winds or stay the lighting with song. No. Ambitious men must be restrained by the public morality: when they rise up to do evil, they must find themselves standing alone. Morality rests on religion. If you destroy the foundation, the superstructure must fall. In a world of error, of temptation, of seduction; in a world where crimes often triumph, and virtue is scourged with scorpions,—in such a world, certainly, the hope of a hereafter is necessary to cheer and to animate. Leave, us, then, the consolations of religion. Leave to man, to frail and feeble man, the comfort of knowing, that, when he gratifies his immortal soul with deeds of justice, of kindness, and of mercy, he is rescuing his happiness from final dissolution and laying it up in Heaven ...

Standing in this place, sacred to truth, I dare not undertake to assure you that your liberties and your happiness may be lost. Men are subject to men's misfortunes. If an angel should be winged from Heaven, on an errand of mercy to our country, the first accents that would glow on his lips would be, Beware! Be cautious! You have everything to lose; you have nothing to gain. We live under the only government that ever existed which was framed by the unrestrained and deliberate consultations of the people. Miracles do not cluster. That which happened but once in six thousand years cannot be expected to happen often. Such government, once gone, might leave a void, to be filled, for ages, with revolution and tumult, riot and despotism. The history of the world is before us. It rises like an immense column, on which we may see inscribed the soundest maxims of political experience. These maxims should be treasured in our memories and written on our hearts . . . .

8

The American and French Revolutions

Lemuel Shaw, 1815

> *At the invitation of the citizens of Boston, Lemuel Shaw (1781–1861)—politician, lawyer, and future Chief Justice of the Massachusetts Supreme Court—delivered the following oration for the Fourth of July, 1815. In his address, Shaw compared the principles of the American Revolution to those of the French Revolution (which had commenced in 1789 and ended with the exile of Napoleon in 1814), and he warned against a sectional break up of the American Union.*

Designated by your municipal government, to assist in the services of the day, permit me, my fellow citizens, to congratulate you on another peaceful return of this anniversary, to exult with you in the interesting events, which it is designed to commemorate, and to retrace some of those feelings, manners and principles, which led to the declaration, and terminated in the triumphant establishment of our national independence. In performing this annual duty, allow time to solicit your most liberal indulgence. Recollecting how often you have been delighted with the glowing eloquence of my predecessors, I should utterly despair of success, were I not supported by the conviction, that the subject, apparently exhausted as it is, will never cease to be dear to the heart of every patriotic American. The lapse of time, whilst it may impair something of our original interest in the event, will confirm the principles of the revolution, and add weight to the lessons of wisdom, which it is calculated to impart . . .

By her declaration of independence and the principles expressly asserted or practically maintained by the constitution of her general government, and those of the several states, American has hazarded a bold attempt to establish a more perfect state of civil liberty and popular government, than the experience of the world has yet witnessed. The whole form and theory of her polity is founded on the principle, that the happiness of the people is the only legitimate object of government. They profess to guarantee to every individual, by fixed and permanent laws, the security of life, liberty, property, reputation and the pursuit of happiness, the right of free discussion upon every subject, by speech, writing and printing, the most unlimited exercise of the rights of conscience and of worship, and an entire and absolute exemption from all exercise of arbitrary power . . .

Military corruption or political depravity, the mad ambition and profligacy of rulers, or the degeneracy and debasement of the people, can alone eradicate the principles of liberty, blast the hopes of refinement, and bring back another age of darkness and barbarism. How solemn all admonition is this, my countrymen, how powerful an appeal to the heart of the patriot and philanthropist, to cherish the national and manly virtues, to banish all narrow, selfish views, to frown with indignation on the arts, and frauds, and intrigues of designing men, to cultivate the higher powers of intellect, to cherish the nobler feelings of patriotism, to diffuse useful and practical truth, in order to qualify and sustain us for the high career of national glory, which Providence has opened to our view. The occasion requires, that we should take a nearer view of the actual condition of our country, with reference both to its external relations and internal policy. The happy return of peace, for which our gratitude is so justly due to the protecting mercy of Heaven, having relieved us from suffering, agitation and alarm, allows us leisure to survey our condition, and prepare for our future destiny. Although a season like this, divests the political interests of the day, of that deep and earnest interest, which we feel under the pressure of more trying circumstances, the occasion will be improved by the wise and reflecting for calm deliberation. But how painfully does this scene of tranquility and repose contrast with the deep and awful note of preparation, which reaches us from Europe. Oh who can cast a momentary view O'er the vine-covered hills and gay regions of France, and not turn away with mingled emotions of horror, indignation and pity. Twenty-five years have now elapsed since the French revolution burst upon the view of the astonished world, and opened a scene of wretchedness and of crimes, of atheism and profligacy, utterly without a parallel in the annals of history. The American revolution has suffered an irreparable injury by being compared with that of France. But they differed not less in principle and in object, than in the means, with which they were conducted, and the manner, in which they were terminated. The leaders of the French revolution, manifesting an utter disregard to all principle in their measures, and sincerity in their professions, actuated by deadly hatred to all that was eminent and respectable in character, or amiable and elegant in manners, or fixed and settled in the institutions of society, and instigated by a boundless ambition, readily seized on the enthusiasm themselves had excited, to gratify their malignant passions. After a few feverish years of liberty, this horrible revolution terminated, as all reflecting men had foreseen that it must terminate, in a government of physical force, a cruel, ferocious military despotism. The rule of Bonaparte was little more than a continued scene of oppression, outrage, and contempt of social rights. No spot within the extent of his empire was too elevated or too humble to be the object of his regard. The palace and the cottage, the sanctuary of the church, the halls of science, the universities and schools, the counting-house of the merchant the work-shop of the artisan, the hallowed abode of domestic retirement, incessantly felt and lamented his oppressive influence. Had Bonaparte been content to confine the sphere of his relentless tyranny to France alone, the world would have had less reason to complain. It would have been a question for high minded Frenchmen alone, whether they would submit in silence to the total subversion of their liberties, or take measures for their emancipation. But Bonaparte was ambitious; and with the most power military ever brought to act at the will of one man, grasped at universal conquest. Europe bore witness, not only to his ambition, but its fatal success. Nearly every capital of continental Europe had submitted successively to the triumph of his arms. These indeed were times which appalled the firmest minds. They began to apprehend, that the sun of freedom had set forever, and that society was destined to sink back into darkness and barbarism. But suddenly the light of hope and of joy burst with splendor from the north, the conqueror is defeated, his hordes scattered, himself a fugitive. Such was the joyful acclamation, which all Europe responded. The fatal blow indeed was struck. After a few vain and fruitless struggles, the proud and haughty conqueror was glad to purchase his life by the humiliating surrender of his throne, and to seek in the little island of Elba, a humble asylum from the contempt and execration of mankind. We, my friends, did rejoice, most sincerely and cordially rejoice in this series of events, not merely because we had suffered injuries and indignities from the despot, nor because his fall would promote our prosperity, but because we considered it as the triumph of the cause of justice, or liberty and humanity, and because we sincerely believed, that it would restore happiness to France, and safety to the world . . .

What is to be the future conduct of the United States, is a subject of most interesting inquiry . . . Should the time ever come, when one portion of the union, influenced by a mistaken estimate of local interests, governed by false views and unworthy prejudices, shall entertain sentiments, and adopt measures hostile to the rights and liberties of another, should faction, seizing the high places of government, with the aid of a numerical majority, endeavor to give to usurpation and injustice the forms of law, should the spirit and design of the constitution be openly perverted to lend its sanction to these measures, should all reasonable means of redress prove unavailing, and such a course be systematically persisted in, nothing would remain to the injured party, but to prepare deliberately for the crisis, and to exclaim in the spirit of the declaration of independence, perish the union, perish the constitution, they have ceased to preserve our liberties and our rights. From such a crisis, may God in mercy long preserve our beloved country. It belongs to the people of the United States to cherish the union, in the spirit with which it was formed, as the means of justice, of security, of safety and happiness to all. Let the great sections and divisions of the United States banish the local prejudices and narrow jealousies, which affect vulgar and superficial minds, and let them learn to respect the character, the views, the interests, and feelings of each other. Experience has shewn that much of that prejudice is unfounded; its consequences are obvious and lamented. Between the different great sections of the union, it would be easy to demonstrate an intimate community of interest, but I forbear. To the integrity, the good sense and intelligence of the American people their happiness is entrusted. Americans, let me once more remind you of your illustrious origin and your high distinction. Oh stain not the purity of your youthful virtue, tarnish not the luster of your early fame. Banish from our counsels the traitors, who would poison your sentiments and abuse your confidence. Impress on the minds of your children an early and ardent love of country. Cherish a rational character, cultivate the national virtues, so shall you prove to a remote posterity, that the solid fabric of freedom and independence, which you have now raised, is but the foundation of a loftier monument of national glory, happiness, and fame.

9

American Principles

John Quincy Adams, 1821

John Quincy Adams (1767–1848) gave the following Fourth of July oration while serving as Secretary of State under President James Monroe. In his address, Adams argued that the "principles" in the preamble to the Declaration—rather than the particular charges against the King—were the proper objects of celebration on the Fourth of July. In terms of foreign policy, Adams warned against participation in European wars and maintained that, consistent with the principles in the Declaration, America ought to be "the well-wisher to the freedom and independence of all" but "the champion and vindicator only of her own."

. . . Then it was that the thirteen United Colonies of North America, by their delegates in Congress assembled, exercising the first act of sovereignty by a right ever inherent in the people, but never to be restored to, save the awful crisis when civil society is solved into its first elements, declared themselves free and independent states; and two days afterwards, in justification of that act, issued this UNANIMOUS DECLARATION OF THE THIRTEEN STATES OF AMERCA . . . It is not, let me repeat, fellow-citizens, it is not the long enumeration of intolerable wrongs concentrated in this declaration; it is not the melancholy catalogue of alternate oppression and intreaty, of reciprocated indignity and remonstrance, upon which, in the celebration of this anniversary, your memory delights to dwell. Nor is it yet that the justice of your cause was vindicated by the God of battles; that in a conflict of seven years, the history of the war by which you maintained that declaration, became the history of the civilized world; that the unanimous voice of enlightened Europe and the verdict of an after age have sanctioned your assumption of sovereign power, and that the name of your Washington is enrolled upon the records of time, first in the glorious line of heroic virtue. It is not that the monarch himself, who had been your oppressor, was compelled to recognize you as a sovereign and independent people, and that the nation, whose feelings of fraternity for you had slumbered in the lap of pride, was awakened in the arms of humiliation to your equal and no longer contested rights. The primary purpose of this declaration, the proclamation to the world of the causes of our revolution, is "with the years beyond the flood." It is of no more interest to us than the chastity of Lucretia, or the apple on the head of the child of Tell. Little less than forty years have revolved since the struggle for independence was closed; another generation has arisen; and in the assembly of nations our republic is already a matron of mature age. The cause of your independence is no longer on trial. The final sentence upon it has long since been passed upon earth and ratified in heaven. The interest, which in this paper has survived the occasion upon which it was issued; the interest which is of every age and every clime; the interest which quickens with the lapse of years, spreads as it grows old, and brightens as it recedes, is in the principles which it proclaims. It was the first solemn declaration by a nation of the only legitimate foundation of civil government. It was the corner stone of a new fabric, destined to cover the surface of the globe. It demolished at a stroke the lawfulness of all governments founded upon conquest. It swept away all the rubbish of accumulated centuries of servitude. It announced in practical form to the world the transcendent truth of the unalienable sovereignty of the people. It proved that the social compact was no figment of the imagination; but a real, solid, and sacred bond of the social union. From the day of this declaration, the people of North America were no longer the fragment of a distant empire, imploring justice and mercy from an inexorable master in another hemisphere. They were no longer children appealing in vain to the sympathies of a heartless mother; no longer subjects leaning upon the shattered columns of royal promises, and invoking the faith of parchment to secure their rights. They were a nation, asserting as a right, and maintaining by war, its own existence. A nation was born in a day. "How many ages hence Shall this their lofty scene be acted o'er in states unborn, and accents yet unknown?" It will be acted o'er, fellow-citizens, but it can never be repeated. It stands, and must forever stand alone, a beacon on the summit of the mountain, to which all the inhabitants of the earth may turn their eyes for a genial and saving light, till time shall be lost in eternity, and this globe itself dissolve, nor leave a wreck behind. It stands forever, a light of admonition to the rulers of men; a light of salvation and redemption to the oppressed. So long as this planet shall be inhabited by human beings, so long as man shall be of a social nature, so long as government shall be necessary to the great moral purposes of society, and so long as it shall be abused to the purposes of oppression, so long shall this declaration hold out to the sovereign and to the subject the extent and the boundaries of their respective rights and duties; founded in the laws of nature and of nature's God. Five and forty years have passed away since this Declaration was issued by our fathers; and here are we, fellow-citizens, assembled in the full enjoyment of its fruits, to bless the Author of our being for the bounties of his providence, in casting our lot in this favored land; to remember with effusions of gratitude the sages who put forth, and the heroes who bled for the establishment of this Declaration; and, by the communion of soul in the reperusal and hearing of this instrument, to renew the genuine Holy Alliance of its principles, to recognize them as eternal truths, and to pledge ourselves and bind our posterity to a faithful and undeviating adherence to them. Fellow-citizens, our fathers have been faithful to them before us. When the little band of their Delegates, "with a firm reliance on the protection of Divine Providence, for the support of this declaration, mutually pledged to each other their lives, their fortunes, and their sacred honor," from every dwelling, street, and square of your populous cities, it was re-echoed with shouts of joy and gratulation! And if the silent language of the heart could have been heard, every hill upon the surface of this continent which had been trodden by the foot of civilized man, every valley in which the toil of your fathers had opened a paradise upon the wild, would have rung, with one accordant voice, louder than the thunders, sweeter than the harmonies of the heavens, with the solemn and responsive words, "We swear." The pledge has been redeemed . . .

In the progress of forty years since the acknowledgment of our independence, we have gone through many modifications of internal government, and through all the vicissitudes of peace and war, with other mighty nations. But never, never for a moment have the great principles, consecrated by the Declaration of this day, been renounced or abandoned. And now, friends and countrymen, if the wise and learned philosophers of the older world, the first observers of mutation and aberration, the discoverers of maddening ether and invisible planets, the inventors of Congreve rockets and shrapnel shells, should find their hearts disposed to inquire, what has America done for the benefit of mankind? Let our answer be this—America, with the same voice which spoke herself into existence as a nation, proclaimed to mankind the inextinguishable rights of human nature, and the only lawful foundations of government. America, in the assembly of nations, since her admission among them, has invariably, though often fruitlessly, held forth to them the hand of honest friendship, of equal freedom, of generous reciprocity. She has uniformly spoken among them, though often to heedless and often to disdainful ears, the language of equal liberty, equal justice, and equal rights. She has, in the lapse of nearly half a century, without a single exception, respected the independence of other nations, while asserting and maintaining her own. She has abstained form interference in the concerns of others, even when the conflict has been for principles to which she clings, as to the last vital drip that visits the heart. She has seen that probably for centuries to come, all the contests of that Aceldama, the European World, will be contests between inveterate power, and emerging right. Wherever the standard of freedom and independence has been or shall be unfurled, there will her heart, her benedictions and her prayers be. But she goes not abroad in search of monsters to destroy. She is the well-wisher to the freedom and independence of all. She is the champion and vindicator only of her own. She will recommend the general cause, by the countenance of her voice, and the benignant sympathy of her example. She well knows that by once enlisting under other banners than her own, were they even the banners of foreign independence, she would involve herself, beyond the power of extrication, in all the wars of interest and intrigue, of individual avarice, envy, ambition, which assume the colors and usurp the standard of freedom. The fundamental maxims of her policy would insensibly change from liberty to force. The frontlet upon her brows would not longer beam with the ineffable splendor of freedom and independence; but in its stead would soon be substituted an imperial diadem, flashing in false and tarnished luster the murky radiance of dominion and power. She might become the dictatress of the world: she would be no longer the ruler of her own spirit. Stand forth, ye champions of Britannia, ruler of the waves Stand forth, ye chivalrous knights of chartered liberties and the rotten borough! Enter the lists, ye boasters of inventive genius! Ye mighty masters of the palette and the brush! Ye improvers upon the sculpture of Elgin marbles! Ye spawners of fustian romance lascivious lyrics! Come, and inquire what has American done for the benefit of mankind! In the half century which has elapsed since the declaration of American independence, what have you done for the benefit of mankind? . . . Her glory is not dominion, but liberty. Her march is the march of mind. She has a spear and a shield; but the motto upon her shield is Freedom, Independence, Peace. This has been her declaration: this has been, as far as her necessary intercourse with the rest of mankind would permit, her practice. My countrymen, fellow-citizens, and friends; could that Spirit, which dictated the Declaration we have this day read, that Spirit, which "prefers before all temples the upright heart and pure," at this moment descend from his habitation in the skies and within this hall, in language audible to mortal ears, address each of us, here assembled, our beloved country, Britannia ruler of the waves, and every individual among the sceptered lords of humankind; his words would be, "Go though and do likewise!"

10

Fifty Years Later

Thomas Jefferson, 1826

During the semi-centennial of American Independence, Thomas Jefferson reflected on the influence of the Declaration, and he celebrated what he considered to be the growing acceptance of "the palpable truth, that the mass of mankind has not been born with saddles on their backs, nor a favored few booted and spurred, ready to ride them, legitimately, by the grace of god."

Monticello June 24.
Respected Sir

The kind invitation I receive from you on the part of the citizens of the city of Washington, to be present with them at their celebration of the 50th. anniversary of American independence; as one of the surviving signers of an instrument pregnant with our own, and the fate of the world, is most flattering to myself, and heightened by the honorable accompaniment proposed for the comfort of such a journey. it adds sensibly to the sufferings of sickness, to be deprived by it of a personal participation in the rejoicings of that day. but acquiescence is a duty, under circumstances not placed among those we are permitted to controul. I should, indeed, with peculiar delight, have met and exchanged there congratulations personally with the small band, the remnant of that host of worthies, who joined with us on that day, in the bold and doubtful election we were to make for our country, between submission or the sword; and to have enjoyed with them the consolatory fact, that our fellow citizens, after half a century of experience and prosperity, continue to approve the choice we made. may it be to the world, what I believe it will be, (to some parts sooner, to others later, but finally to all,) the Signal of arousing men to burst the chains, under which monkish ignorance and superstition had persuaded them to bind themselves, and to assume the blessings & security of self-government. that form which we have substituted, restores the free right to the unbounded exercise of reason and freedom of opinion. all eyes are opened, or opening, to the rights of man. the general spread of the light of science has already laid open to every view. the palpable truth, that the mass of mankind has not been born with saddles on their backs, nor a favored few booted and spurred, ready to ride them legitimately, by the grace of god. these are grounds of hope for others. for ourselves, let the annual return of this day forever refresh our recollections of these rights, and an undiminished devotion to them.

I will ask permission here to express the pleasure with which I should have met my ancient neighbors of the City of Washington and of it's vicinities, with whom I passed so many years of a pleasing social intercourse; an intercourse which so much relieved the anxieties of the public cares, and left impressions so deeply engraved in my affections, as never to be forgotten. with my regret that ill health forbids me the gratification of an acceptance, be pleased to receive for yourself, and those for whom you write, the assurance of my highest respect and friendly attachments.

Th. Jefferson

11

The Lives and Characters of Thomas Jefferson and John Adams

William Wirt, 1826

It is one of the remarkable coincidences of history that Thomas Jefferson and John Adams both died on the Declaration's fiftieth anniversary—July 4, 1826. "Thomas Jefferson survives," Adams is reported to have said on his deathbed, unaware that Jefferson had passed just a few hours earlier. On October 19, 1826, United States Attorney General William Wirt (1772–1834) gave the following address in the Hall of Representatives to commemorate the lives of Jefferson and Adams.

The scenes which have been lately passing in our country, and of which this meeting is a continuance, are full of moral instruction. They hold up to the world a lesson of wisdom by which all may profit, if Heaven shall grant them the discretion to turn it to its use. The spectacle, in all its parts, has, indeed, been most solemn and impressive; and, though the first impulse be now past, the time has not yet come, and never will it come, when we can contemplate it, without renewed emotion. In the structure of their characters; in the course of their action; in the striking coincidences which marked their high career; in the lives and in the deaths of the illustrious men, whose virtues and services we have met to commemorate—and in that voice of admiration and gratitude which has since burst, with one accord, from the twelve millions of freemen who people these States, there is a moral sublimity which overwhelms the mind, and hushes all its powers into silent amazement!

The European, who should have heard the sound without apprehending the cause, would be apt to inquire, "What is the meaning of all this? What had these men done to elicit this unanimous and splendid acclamation?" Why has the whole American nation risen up, as one man, to do them honor, and offer them this enthusiastic homage of the heart? Were they mighty warriors, and was the peal that we have heard, the shout of victory? Were they great commanders, returning from their distant conquests, surrounded with the spoils of war, and was this the sound of their triumphal procession? Were they covered with martial glory in any form, and was this the noisy wave of the multitude rolling back at their approach? Nothing of all this: No, they were peaceful and aged patriots, who, having served their country together, through their long and useful lives, had now sunk together to the tomb. They had not fought battles; but they had formed and moved the great machinery of which battles were only a small, and, comparatively, trivial consequence. They had not commanded armies; but they had commanded the master springs of the nation, on which all its great political, as well as military movements depended. By the wisdom and energy of their counsels, and by the potent mastery of their spirits, they had contributed pre-eminently to produce a mighty Revolution, which has changed the aspect of the world. A Revolution which, in onehalf of that world, has already restored man to his "long lost liberty," and government to its only legitimate object, the happiness of the People: and, on the other hemi-sphere, has thrown a light so strong, that even the darkness of despotism is beginning to recede. Compared with the solid glory of an achievement like this, what are battles, and what are the pomp of war, but the poor and fleeting pageants of a theatre? What were the selfish and petty strides of Alexander, to conquer a little section of a savage world, compared with this generous, this magnificent advance towards the emancipation of the entire world! And this, be it remembered, has been the fruit of intellectual exertion! The triumph of mind! What a proud testimony does it bear to the character of our nation, that they are able to make a proper estimate of services like these! That while, in other countries, the senseless mob fall down, in stupid admiration, before the bloody wheels of the conqueror—even of the conqueror by accident—in this, our People rise, with one accord, to pay their homage to intellect and virtue! What a cheering pledge does it give of the stability of our institutions, that while abroad, the yet benighted multitude are prostrating themselves before the idols which their own hands have fashioned into Kings, here, in this land of the free, our People are every where starting up with one impulse, to follow with their acclamations the ascending spirits of the great Fathers of the Republic! This is a spectacle of which we may be permitted to be proud. It honors our country no less than the illustrious dead. And could those great Patriots speak to us from the tomb, they would tell us that they have more pleasure in the testimony which these honors bear to the character of their country, than in that which they bear to their individual services. They now see as they were seen, while in the body, and know the nature of the feeling from which these honors flow. It is love for love. It is the gratitude of an enlightened nation to the noblest order of benefactors. It is the glory with the aspiration of a generous spirit. Who would not prefer this living tomb in the hearts of his countrymen, to the proudest mausoleum that the Genius of Sculpture could erect! Man has been said to be the creature of accidental position. The cast of his character has been thought to depend, materially, on the age, the country, and the circumstances, in which he has lived. To a considerable extent, the remark is, no doubt, true. Cromwell, had he been born in a Republic, might have been "guiltless of his country's blood;" and, but for those civil commotions which had wrought his great mind into tempest, Milton might have rested "mute and inglorious." The occasion is, doubtless, necessary to develop the talent, whatsoever it may be; but the talent must exist, in embryo at least, or no occasion can quicken it into life. And it must exist, too, under the check of strong virtues; or the same occasion that quickens it into life, will be extremely apt to urge it on to crime. The hero who finished his career at St. Helena, extraordinary as he was, is a far more common character in the history of the world, than he who sleeps in our neighborhood, embalmed in his country's tears—or than those whom we have now met to mourn and to honor.

Jefferson and Adams were great men by nature. Not great and eccentric minds "shot madly from their spheres" to affright the world and scatter pestilence in their course; but minds whose strong and steady light, restrained within their proper orbits by the happy poise of their characters, came to cheer and to gladden a world that had been buried for ages in political night. They were heaven-called avengers of degraded man. They came to lift him to the station for which God had formed him, and to put to flight those idiot superstitions with which tyrants had contrived to inthrall his reason and his liberty. And that Being who had sent them upon this mission, had fitted them, pre-eminently for his glorious work. He filled their hearts with a love of country which burned strong within them, even in death. He gave them a power of understanding which no sophistry could baffle, no art elude; and a moral heroism which no dangers could appal. Careless of themselves, reckless of all personal consequences, trampling under foot that petty ambition of office and honor which constitutes the master passion of little minds, they bent all their powers to the task for which they had been delegated—the freedom of their beloved country, and the restoration of fallen man. They rested not until they had accomplished their work at home, and given such an impulse to the great ocean of mind, that they saw the waves rolling on to the farthest shore, before they were called to their reward. And then left the world, hand in hand, as they rose, in the success of their labors . . .

Hitherto, my fellow citizens, the Fourth of July had been celebrated among us, only as the anniversary of our independence, and its votaries had been merely human beings. But at its last recurrence—the great Jubilee of the nation—the anniversary, it may well be termed, of the liberty of man—Heaven, itself, mingled visibly in the celebration, and hallowed the day anew by a double apotheosis. Is there one among us to whom this language seems too strong? Let him recall his own feelings, and the objection will vanish. When the report first reached us, of the death of the great man whose residence was nearest, who among us was not struck with the circumstance that he should have been removed on the day of his own highest glory? And who, after the first shock of the intelligence had passed, did not feel a thrill of mournful delight at the characteristic beauty of the close of such a life. But while our bosoms were yet swelling with admiration at this singularly beautiful coincidence, when the second report immediately followed, of the death of the great sage of Quincy, on the same day—I appeal to your selves—is there a voice that was not hushed, is there a heart that did not quail, at this close manifestation of the hand of Heaven in our affairs! Philosophy, recovered of her surprise, may affect to treat the coincidence as fortuitous. But Philosophy herself was mute, at the moment, under the pressure of the feeling that these illustrious men had rather been translated, than had died. It is in vain to tell us that men die by thousands every day in the year, all over the world. The wonder is not that two men have died on the same day, but that two such men, after having performed so many and such splendid services in the cause of liberty—after the multitude of other coincidences which seem to have linked their destinies together—after having lived so long together , the objects of their country's joint veneration—after having been spared to witness the great triumph of their toils at home—and looked together from Pisgah's top, on the sublime effect of that grand impulse which they had given to the same glorious cause throughout the world, should, on this fiftieth anniversary of the day on which they had ushered that cause into light, be both caught up to Heaven, together, in the midst of their raptures! Is there a being, of heart so obdurate and sceptical, as not to feel the hand and hear the voice of Heaven in this wonderful dispensation? And may we not, with reverence, interpret its language? Is it not this? "These are my beloved servants, with whom I am well pleased. They have finished the work for which I sent them into the world: and are now called to their reward. Go ye, and do likewise!" One circumstance, alone, remains to be noticed. In a private memorandum found among some other obituary papers and relics of Mr. Jefferson, is a suggestion, in case a memorial over him should ever be thought of, that a granite obelisk, of small dimensions, should be erected, with the following inscription: HERE LIES BURIED THOMAS JEFFERSON, Author of the Declaration of Independence, Of the Statutes of Virginia for religious freedom, And Father of the University of Virginia. All the long catalogue of his great, and splendid, and glorious services, reduced to this brief and modest summary! Thus lived and died our sainted Patriots! May their spirits still continue to hover over their countrymen, inspire all their counsels, and guide them in the same virtuous and noble path! And may that God, in whose hands are the issues of all things, confirm and perpetuate, to us, the inestimable boon which, through their agency, he has bestowed; and make our Columbia, the bright exemplar, for all the struggling sons of liberty around the globe!

II
THE DECLARATION IN A HOUSE DIVIDED

12

Petition for Freedom

"A Great Number of Blackes," 1777

> *Prentice Hall (1735–1807), a leader of the free black community in Boston, submitted the following petition to the Massachusetts legislature on January 13, 1777. In the petition, "A Great Number of Blackes detained in a State of Slavery" asserted that "every principle" of the American Revolution "Pleads Stronger than A thousand arguments" in favor of the abolition of slavery in America.*

The petition of A Great Number of Blackes detained in a State of Slavery in the Bowels of a free & christian Country Humbly shuwith that your Petitioners Apprehend that Thay have in Common with all other men a Natural and Unaliable Right to that freedom which the Grat Parent of the Unavese hath Bestowed equalley on all menkind and which they have Never forfuted by Any Compact or Agreement whatever—but thay wher Unjustly Dragged by the hand of cruel Power from their Derest frinds and sum of them Even torn from the Embraces of their tender Parents—from A populous Plasant And plentiful cuntry And in Violation of Laws of Nature and off Nations And in defiance of all the tender feelings of humanity Brough hear Either to Be sold Like Beast of Burthen & Like them Condemnd to Slavery for Life—among A People Profesing the Religion of Jesus A people Not Insensible of the Secrets of Rationable Being Nor without spirit to Resent the unjust endeavours of others to Reduce them to A state of Bondage and Subjection your honouer Need not to be informed that A Life of Slavery Like that of your Petioners Deprived of Every social Priviledge of Every thing Requiset to Render Life Tolable is far worse then Nonexistance. In imitation of Lawdable Example of the Good People of these States your petiononers have Long and Patiently waited the Evnt of petition after petition By them presented to the Legislative Body of this state And cannot but with Grief Reflect that their Success hath ben but too similar they Cannot but express their Astonisments that It has Never Bin Consirdered that Every Principle from which Amarica has Acted in the Cours Of their unhappy Deficultes with Great Briton Pleads Stronger than A thousand arguments in favowrs of Your petioners thay therfor humble Beseech your Honours to give this petion its due weight & considerration and cause an act of the Legislatur to be past Wherby they may Be Restored to the Enjoyments of that Which is the Naturel Right of all men—and their—Children who wher Born in this Land of Liberty may not be heald as Slaves after they arive at the age of Twenty one years so may the Inhabitance of thes State No longer chargeable with the inconsistancey of acting themselves the part which thay condem and oppose in Others Be prospered in their present Glorious Struggle for Liberty and have those Blessing to them &c.

13

The Constitution and Slavery

Luther Martin, 1787

> *Luther Martin (1748–1826) was a Maryland delegate to the Constitutional Convention in 1787 and a leading opponent of ratification. In the following speech, delivered to the Maryland legislature in 1787, Martin argued that the treatment of slavery in the Constitution was grossly inconsistent with the ideals in the Declaration of Independence.*

By the *ninth* section of this article [i.e., U.S. Const., Art. I –ed.], the importation of such persons as any of the States now existing, shall think proper to admit, shall not be prohibited prior to the year one thousand eight hundred and eight, but a duty may be imposed on such importation not exceeding ten dollars for each person.

The design of this clause is to prevent the general government from prohibiting the importation of slaves, but the same reasons which caused them to strike out the word *"national,"* and not admit the word *"stamps,"* influenced them here to guard against the word *"slaves,"* they anxiously sought to avoid the admission of expressions which might be odious in the ears of Americans, although they were willing to admit into their system those *things* which the *expressions* signified: And hence it is, that the clause is so worded, as really to authorise the general government to impose a duty of ten dollars on every foreigner who comes into a State to become a citizen, whether he comes *absolutely free*, or *qualifiedly* so as a servant; although this is contrary to the design of the framers, and the duty was only meant to extend to the importation of *slaves*.

This clause was the subject of a great diversity of sentiment in the convention:—as the system was reported by the committee of detail, the provision was general, that such importation should not be prohibited, without confining it to any particular period. This was rejected by eight States—Georgia, South-Carolina, and I think North-Carolina voting for it.

We were then told by the delegates of the two first of those States, that their States would never agree to a system which put it in the power of the general government to prevent the importation of slaves, and that they, as delegates from those States, must withhold their assent from such a system.

A committee of one member from each State was chosen by ballot, to take this part of the system under their consideration, and to endeavour to agree upon some report, which should reconcile those States; to this committee also was referred the following proposition, which had been reported by the committee of detail, to wit, "No *navigation act* shall be passed without the assent of *two thirds* of the members present in each house;" a proposition which the *staple* and *commercial* States were solicitous to *retain*, lest their *commerce* should be placed too much under the power of the *eastern* States, but which these last States were as anxious to *reject*.—This committee, of which also I had the honour to be a member, met and took under their consideration the subjects committed to them; I found the *eastern* States, notwithstanding their *aversion to slavery*, were very willing to indulge the southern States, at least with a temporary liberty to prosecute the *slave trade*, provided the southern States would in their turn gratify them, by laying no *restriction* on *navigation acts*; and after a very little time, the committee by a great majority, agreed on a report, by which the general government was to be prohibited from preventing the importation of slaves for a limited time, and the restrictive clause relative to navigation acts was to be omitted.

This report was adopted by a majority of the convention, but not without considerable opposition.—It was said, that we had but just assumed a place among independent nations, in consequence of our opposition to the attempts of Great-Britain to *enslave us;* that this opposition was grounded upon the *preservation of those rights,* to which God and Nature had entitled *us,* not in *particular,* but in *common* with *all the rest of mankind*—That we had *appealed* to the *Supreme being* for his *assistance,* as the *God of freedom,* who could not but *approve* our efforts to preserve the *rights* which he had thus *imparted to his creatures;* that now, when we scarcely had risen from our *knees,* from *supplicating* his *aid* and *protection*—in *forming our government* over *a free people,* a government formed pretendedly on the *principles* of *liberty* and for its *preservation,*—in *that* government to have a provision, not only putting it out *of its power* to *restrain* and *prevent* the *slave trade,* but *even encouraging that most infamous traffic,* by giving the *States power* and *influence* in the *union, in proportion* as they *cruelly and wantonly sport with the rights of their fellow creatures,* ought to be considered as a *solemn mockery of,* and *insult to, that God* whose protection we had then implored, and could not fail to hold us up in *detestation,* and render us *contemptible* to every *true friend* of liberty in the world. It was said, it ought to be considered that *national crimes* can *only be, and frequently are, punished* in this world by *national punishments,* and that the *continuance* of the slave trade, and thus giving it a *national sanction* and *encouragement,* ought to be considered as *justly exposing* us to the *displeasure* and *vengeance* of *Him,* who is equal Lord of all, and who views with equal eye, the poor *African slave* and his *American master!*

It was urged, that by this system, we were giving the general government full and absolute power to regulate commerce, under which general power it would have a right to *restrain, or totally prohibit* the *slave trade:* it must therefore, appear to the world absurd and disgraceful to the last degree, that we should *except from* the exercise of that power, the *only branch* of *commerce* which is *unjustifiable in its nature,* and *contrary* to the *rights of mankind*—That on the contrary, we ought *rather to prohibit expressly* in our *constitution,* the *further importation of slaves;* and to *authorise* the general government from time to time, to make such regulations as should be thought most advantageous for the *gradual abolition* of *slavery,* and the *emancipation* of the *slaves* which are already in the States.

That *slavery* is *inconsistent* with the *genius* of *republicanism,* and has a tendency to *destroy* those *principles* on which it is *supported,* as it *lessens the sense* of the *equal rights* of *mankind,* and habituates us to *tyranny* and *oppression.* It was further urged, that by this system of government, every State is to be protected both from *foreign invasion* and from *domestic insurrections;* that from this consideration, it was of the *utmost importance* it should have a power to restrain the importation of slaves, since in proportion as the number of slaves were increased in any State, in the same proportion the State is *weakened* and *exposed* to foreign invasion, or domestic insurrection, and by *so much the less* will it be able to protect itself against *either;* and therefore will by so much the more, want aid from, and be a burthen to, the union. It was further said, that as in this system we were giving the general government a power under the idea of national character, or national interest, to regulate even our *weights* and *measures,* and have prohibited all possibility of *emitting paper money,* and *passing instalment laws, &c.* It must appear still more extraordinary, that we should prohibit the government from interfering with the slave trade, than which *nothing* could so *materially affect* both our *national honour* and *interest.*—These reasons influenced me both on the committee and in convention, most decidedly to oppose and vote against the clause, as it now makes a part of the system.

You will perceive, Sir, not only that the general government is prohibited from interfering in the slave trade *before* the year eighteen hundred and eight, but that there is no provision in the constitution that it shall *afterwards* be prohibited, nor any security that such prohibition will ever take place; and I think there is great reason to believe, that if the importation of slaves is permitted until the year eighteen hundred and eight, it will not be prohibited afterwards: At *this time* we do not generally hold this commerce in so *great* abhorrence as we have done—When our liberties were at stake, we *warmly* felt for the *common rights of men*—The danger being thought to be past, which threatened ourselves, we are daily growing *more insensible* to those rights—In those States who have restrained or prohibited the importation of slaves, it is only done by legislative acts which may be repealed—When those States find that they must in their *national character* and *connexion* suffer in the *disgrace*, and share in the *inconveniencies* attendant upon that detestable and iniquitous traffic, they may be desirous also to share in the *benefits* arising from it, and the odium attending it will be greatly effaced by the sanction which is given to it in the general government.

14

Republican Consistency!

William Lloyd Garrison, 1838

> *William Lloyd Garrison (1805–1879) was one of the principal founders of the American Anti-Slavery Society in 1833. On July 4, 1838, Garrison chastised America for betraying her revolutionary principles and deemed the Fourth of July a "great carnival of republican despotism." Garrison further insisted that every slave should learn two important truths: 1) he has a right to freedom, and 2) this right is described as "self-evident" in the Declaration of Independence.*

Fellow Citizens: What a glorious day is this! What a glorious people are we! This is the time-honored *wine*-honored, toast-drinking, powder-wasting, tyrant-killing fourth of July—consecrated, for the last sixty years, to bombast, to falsehood, to impudence, to hypocrisy. It is the great carnival of republican despotism, and of Christian impiety, famous the world over! Since we held it last year, we have kept securely in their chains, the stock of two millions, three hundred thousand slaves we then had on hand, in spite of every effort of fanaticism to emancipate them; and, through the goodness of God, to whom we are infinitely indebted for the divine institution of negro slavery, have been graciously enabled to steal some seventy thousand babes, to increase of that stock, and expect to steal a still greater number before 'another glorious' anniversary shall come round! We have again struck down the freedom of speech in Congress, and utterly banished it from one half of the Union, by the aid of pistols, bowie-knives, and lynch-law. We have also renewedly decided, in both houses of Congress, that the right of petition is not to be allowed to those who are the advocates of immediate and universal emancipation. As to the Indian tribes, we have done the best we could to expel and exterminate them; and the blood upon our hands, and the gore upon our garments, show that our success has almost equaled our wishes. We have driven the Cherokees, at the point of the bayonet, into a distant wilderness, from their abodes of civilization—violated the most solemn treaties ever entered into between man and man—and committed nameless and numberless outrages upon the domestic security and personal rights of these hapless victims,—all for the laudable purpose of getting their lands, that the 'divine institution' of slavery may be extended, and perpetuated to the latest generation, as 'the corner-stone of our republican edifice!' We have trampled all law and order under foot, resolved society into jacobinical clubs, and filled the land with mobs and riots which have ended in arson and murder, in order to show our abhorrence of those who 'plead for justice in the name of humanity, and according to the law of the living God.' Hail Columbia! happy land! Hail, the return of the fourth of July, that we may perjure ourselves afresh, in solemnly invoking heaven and earth to witness, that 'we hold these truths to be self-evident—that all men are created equal; that they are endowed by their Creator with certain inalienable rights; that among these are life, LIBERTY, and the pursuit of happiness!" 'Sound the trumpet—beat the drum!' Let the bells give their merriest peals to the breeze—unfurl every star-spangled banner—thunder mightily, ye, cannon, from every hill-top—and let shouts arise from every plain and valley; for tyrants and their minions shall find no quarter at our hands this day!

I use strong language, and will make no apology for it, on this occasion. In contemplating this subject, no man, who is true to his nature, can speak but in the language of hot displeasure, and caustic irony, and righteous denunciation. Every word will burn like molten lead, and every sentence glow like flaming fire. What are they but a nation of dastards, who, making high pretentions to honesty and a sacred regard for the rights of man, are seen, year after year, openly and shamelessly reducing one-sixth part of the population to chains and slavery, herding the sexes together like beasts, robbing them of the fruits of a toil extorted by a cart-whip, and shutting out from their minds, as far as practicable, all knowledge, both human and divine? The catalogue of our crimes and abominations is without end; and there is nothing that can be tortured into an excuse or apology for their perpetration. Will any man call this declamation? Granted! *The day is consecrated to the declamation*, such as burst from the lips of James Otis, and Joseph Warren, and Patrick Henry, in the days when a three-penny tax upon tea was not to be endured, and when taxation without representation was deemed an outrage worth periling the lives of the colonists to dress!—Declamation? Who will venture to utter that taunt? Is the picture I have sketched overdrawn? Can the most lynx-eyed lawyer detect a single flaw in the indictment? The facts being admitted, metaphasics are rendered needless. As a freeman, I require no argument to convince me, that to enslave or oppress one of my race, is to lift the battle-axe of sedition against the throne of God. Honest, righteous, soul-stirring declamation, against tyranny, is music in my ears. But what harmony is there between the clanking of chains, and the shouts of the forgers of those chains? Between the shrieks of lacerated and bleeding humanity, and the hauntings of those who wield the lash? Between the groans of toil-worn slaves, and the exultations of hypocritical freemen?

I present myself as the advocate of my enslaved countrymen, at a time when their claims cannot be shuffled out of sight, and on occasion which entitles me to a respectful hearing in their behalf. If I am asked to prove their title to liberty, my answer is, that the fourth of July is not a day to be wasted in establishing 'self-evident truths.' In the name of the God, who has made us of one blood, and in whose images we are created; in the name of the Messiah, who came to bind up the broken-hearted, to proclaim liberty to the captives, and the opening of the prison to them that are bound; in the name of the Holy Ghost, whom to despise is to perish; I demand the immediate emancipation of all who are pining in slavery on the American soil, whether they are fattening for the shambles in Maryland and Virginia, or are wasting, as with a pestilent disease, on the cotton and sugar plantations of Alabama and Louisiana; whether they are males or females, young or old, vigorous or infirm. I make this demand, not for the children merely, but the parents also; not for one, but for all; not with restrictions and limitations, but unconditionally. I assert their perfect equality with ourselves, as a part of the human race, and their inalienable right to liberty and the pursuit of happiness. That this demand is founded in justice, and is therefore irresistible, the whole nation is this day acknowledging, as upon oath at the bar of the world. And not until, by a formal vote, the people repudiate the Declaration of Independence as a rotten and dangerous instrument, and cease to keep this festival in honor of liberty, as unworthy of note or remembrance; not until they spike every cannon, and muffle every bell, and disband every procession, and quench every bonfire, and gag every orator; not until they brand Washington, and Adams, and Jefferson, and Hancock, and fanatics and madmen; not until they place themselves again in the condition of colonial subserviency to Great Britain, or transform this republic into an imperial government; not until they cease to point exultingly toward Bunker Hill, and the plains of Concord and Lexington; not, in fine, until they deny the authority of God, and proclaim themselves to be destitute of principle and humanity; will I argue the question, as one of doubtful disputation, on an occasion like this, whether our slaves are entitled to the rights and privileges of freemen. That question is settled irrevocably. There is no man to be found, unless he has a brow of brass and a heart of stone, who will dare to contest it on a day like this. A state of vassalage is pronounced, by universal acclamation, to be such as no man, or body of men, ought to submit to for one moment. I therefore tell the American slaves, that the time for their emancipation is come; that, their own task-masters being witnesses, they are created equal to the rest of mankind, and possess an inalienable right to liberty; and that no man has a right to hold them in bondage. I warn them not to fight for their freedom, both on account of the hopelessness of the effort, and because it is contrary to the will of God; but I tell them, not less emphatically, it is not wrong in them to refuse to wear the yoke of slavery any longer. Let them shed no blood—enter into no conspiracies—raise no murderous revolts; but, whenever and wherever they can break their fetters, God give them the courage to do so! And should they attempt to elope from their house of bondage, and come to the North, may each of them find a cover from the search of the spoiler, and an invincible public sentiment to shield them form the grasp of the kidnapper! Success attend them in their flight to Canada, to touch whose *monarchical* soil insures freedom to every *republican* slave!

Is this preaching sedition? Sedition against what? Not the lives of southern oppressors—for I renew the solemn injunction. 'Shed no blood!'—but against unlawful authority, and barbarous usage, and unrequited toil. If slaveholders are still obstinately bent upon plundering and starving their long-suffering victims, why, let them look well to the consequences. To save them from danger, I am not obligated to suppress the truth, or to stop proclaiming liberty 'throughout all the land, unto all the inhabitants thereof.' No, indeed. There are two important truths, which, as far as practicable, I mean every slave shall be made to understand. The first is, that he has a right to his freedom *now*; the other is that this is recognized as a self-evident truth in the Declaration of American Independence. Sedition, forsooth! Why, what are the American people doing this day? In theory, maintaining the freedom and equality of the human race; and in *practice*, declaring that all tyrants ought to be extirpated from the face of the earth! . . .

15

Amistad Argument

John Quincy Adams, 1841

> *During a voyage from Havana to Puerto Príncipe, Cuba, African captives on board the slave ship "La Amistad" freed themselves, killed the captain of the ship, forced most of the crew overboard, and held two remaining members of the crew hostage. After the ship was found off the coast of New York, the Spanish crew members claimed the Africans as property under a treaty provision that required the return of goods captured from international pirates, and the case made its way to the Supreme Court. Former President John Quincy Adams (1767–1848) was a member of the legal team that represented the Africans; the Van Buren administration sided with Spain. The following excerpt is from Adams's oral argument in the case, which highlighted the principles in the Declaration of Independence. In an opinion authored by Joseph Story, the Court declared that the Africans were entitled to their freedom based on international law and the "eternal principles of justice."*

A COURT OF JUSTICE

In rising to address this Court as one of its attorneys and counselors, regularly admitted at a great distance of time, I feel that an apology might well be expected where I shall perhaps be more likely to exhibit at once the infirmities of age and the inexperience of youth, than to render those services to the individuals whose lives and liberties are at the disposal of this Court which I would most earnestly desire to render. But as I am unwilling to employ one moment of the time of the Court in anything that regards my own personal situation, I shall reserve what few observations I may think necessary to offer as an apology till the close of my argument on the merits of the question.

I therefore proceed immediately to say that, in a consideration of this case, I derive, in the distress I feel both for myself and my clients, consolation from two sources—first, that the rights of my clients to their lives and liberties have already been defended by my learned friend and colleague in so able and complete a manner as leaves me scarcely anything to say, and I feel that such full justice has been done to their interests, that any fault or imperfection of mine will merely be attributed to its true cause; and secondly, I derive consolation from the thought that this Court is a Court of JUSTICE. And in saying so very trivial a thing I should not on any other occasion, perhaps, be warranted in asking the Court to consider what justice is. Justice, as defined in the Institutes of Justinian, nearly 2000 years ago, and as is felt and understood by all who understand human relations and human rights, is—"Constans et perpetua voluntas, jus suum cuique tribuendi."

"The constant and perpetual will to secure to every one HIS OWN right." And in a Court of Justice, where there are two parties present, justice demands that the rights of each party should be allowed to himself, as well as that each party has a right, to be secured and protected by the Court. This observation is important, because I appear here on the behalf of thirty-six individuals, the life and liberty of every one of whom depend on the decision of this Court. The Court, therefore, I trust, in deciding this case, will form no lumping judgment on these thirty-six individuals, but will act on the consideration that the life and the liberty of every one of them must be determined by its decision for himself alone . . .

NO OTHER LAW

One of the Judges who presided in some of the preceding trials, is said to have called this an anomalous case. It is indeed anomalous, and I know of no law, but one which I am not at liberty to argue before this Court, no law, statute or constitution, no code, no treaty, applicable to the proceedings of the Executive or the Judiciary, except that law, (pointing to the copy of the Declaration of Independence, hanging against one of the pillars of the courtroom,) that law, two copies of which are ever before the eyes of your Honors. I know of no other law that reaches the case of my clients, but the law of nature and of Nature's God on which our fathers placed our own national existence. The circumstances are so peculiar, that no code or treaty has provided for such a case. That law, in its application to my clients, I trust will be the law on which the case will be decided by this Court . . .

INDIVIDUAL RIGHTS

That the right to it of every one, is his own—JUS SUMM; and that no greater violation of his official oath to protect and defend the Constitution of the United States, could be committed, than by an order to seize and deliver up at a foreign minister's demand, thirty-six persons, in a mass, under the general denomination of all, the Negroes, late of the Amistad. That he was ignorant, profoundly ignorant of this self-evident truth, inextinguishable till under gilt framed Declarations of Independence shall perish in the general conflagration of the great globe itself. I am constrained to believe—for to that ignorance, the only alternative to account for this order to the Marshal of the District of Connecticut, is willful and corrupt perjury to his official presidential oath. But ignorant or regardless as the President of the United States might be of the self-evident principles of human rights, he was bound to know that he could not lawfully direct the delivery up to a foreign minister, even of slaves, of acknowledged undisputed slaves, in an undefined, unspecified number . . . Lawless and tyrannical; (may it please the Court—Truth, Justice, and the Rights of humankind forbid me to qualify these epithets) . . .

THE PRINCIPLE OF SLAVERY

I now wish simply to refer your Honors to the original principle of slavery as laid down by this champion of the institution. It is given by this writer as a great principle of national law and stands as the foundation of his argument. I wish, if your Honors deem a paper of this kind, published under such circumstances, worthy of consideration in the decision of a case, that your Honors would advert to that principle, and say whether it is a principle recognized by this Court, as the ground on which it will decide cases. "The truth is, that property in man has existed in all ages of the world, and results from the natural state of man, which is war. When God created the first family and gave them the fields of the earth as an inheritance, one of the number, in obedience to the impulses and passions that had been implanted in the human heart, rose and slew his brother. This universal nature of man is alone modified by civilization and law. War, conquest, and force, have produced slavery, and it is state necessity and the internal law of self preservation, that will ever perpetuate and defend it." There is the principle, on which a particular decision is demanded from this Court, by the Official Journal of the Executive, on behalf of the southern states? Is that a principle recognized by this Court? Is it the principle of that DECLARATION? [Here Mr. A. pointed to the Declaration of Independence, two copies of which hang before the eyes of the Judges on the bench.] It is alleged in the Official

Journal, that war gives the right to take the life of our enemy, and that this confers a right to make him a slave, on account of having spared his life. Is that the principle on which these United States stand before the world? That DECLARATION says that every man is "endowed by his Creator with certain inalienable rights," and that among these are life, liberty, and the pursuit of happiness." if these rights are inalienable, they are incompatible with the rights of the victor to take the life of his enemy in war, or to spare his life and make him a slave. If this principle is sound, it reduces to brute force all the rights of man. It places all the sacred relations of life at the power of the strongest. No man has a right to life or liberty, if he has an enemy able to take them from him. There is the principle. There is the whole argument of this paper. Now I do not deny that the only principle upon which a color of right can be attributed to the condition of slavery is by assuming that the natural state of man is war. The bright intellect of the South [i.e., John Calhoun –ed.], clearly saw, that without this principle for a corner stone, he had no foundation for his argument. He assumes it therefore without a blush, as Hobbes assumed it to prove that government and despotism are synonymous words. I will not here discuss the right or the rights of slavery, but I say that the doctrine of Hobbes, that War is the natural state of man, has for ages been exploded, as equally disclaimed and rejected by the philosopher and the Christian. That it is utterly incompatible with any theory of human rights, and especially with the rights which the Declaration of Independence proclaims as self-evident truths. The moment you come, to the Declaration of Independence, that every man has a right to life and liberty, an inalienable right, this case is decided. I ask nothing more in behalf of these unfortunate men, than this Declaration. The opposite principle is laid down, not by an unintelligent or unthinking man, but is given to the public and to this Court, as coming from one of the brightest intellects of the South. Your Honors see what it comes to, when carried out . . .

TAKING LEAVE OF THE BAR

May it please your Honors: On the 7th of February, 1804, now more than thirty-seven years past, my name was entered, and yet stands recorded, on both the rolls, as one of the Attorneys and Counsellors of this Court. Five years later, in February and March, 1809, I appeared for the last time before this Court, in defence of the cause of justice and of important rights, in which many of my fellow-citizens had property to a large amount at stake. Very shortly afterwards, I was called to the discharge of other duties—first in distant lands, and in later years, within our own country, but in different departments of her Government. Little did I imagine that I should ever again be required to claim the right of appearing in the capacity of an officer of this Court; yet such has been the dictate of my destiny—and I appear again to plead the cause of justice, and now of liberty and life, in behalf of many of my fellow men, before that same Court, which in a former age I had addressed in support of rights of property I stand again, I trust for the last time, before the same Court—"hic caestus, artemque repono." I stand before the same Court, but not before the same judges—nor aided by the same associates —nor resisted by the same opponents. As I cast my eyes along those seats of honor and of public trust, now occupied by you, they seek in vain for one of those honored and honorable persons whose indulgence listened then to my voice. Marshall—Cushing—Chase—Washington—Johnson—Livingston— Todd—Where are they? Where is that eloquent statesman and learned lawyer who was my associate counsel in the management of that cause, Robert Goodloe Harper? Where is that brilliant luminary, so long the pride of Maryland and of the American Bar, then my opposing counsel, Luther Martin? Where is the excellent clerk of that day, whose name has been inscribed on the shores of Africa, as a monument of his abhorrence of the African slave-trade, Elias B. Caldwell, Where is the marshal—where are the criers of the Court? Alas! Where is one of the very judges of the Court, arbiters of life and death, before whom I commenced this anxious argument, even now prematurely closed? Where are they all? Gone! Gone! All gone!—Gone from the services which, in their day and generation, they faithfully rendered to their country. From the excellent characters which they sustained in life, so far as I have had the means of knowing, I humbly hope, and fondly trust, that they have gone to receive the rewards of blessedness on high. In taking, then, my final leave of this Bar, and of this Honorable Court, I can only ejaculate a fervent petition to Heaven, that every member of it may go to his final account with as little of earthly frailty to answer for as those illustrious dead, and that you may, every one, after the close of a long and virtuous career in this world, be received at the portals of the next with the approving sentence—"Well done, good and faithful servant; enter thou into the joy of thy Lord."

16

The Cause of the Present Crisis

John C. Calhoun, 1848

> *John C. Calhoun (1782–1850)—Secretary of War, Vice President, and Senator from South Carolina—was one of the leading intellectual defenders of slavery during the antebellum period. In his 1848 speech on territorial policy in Oregon, Calhoun insisted that the real point of conflict between the various sections in the United States was ultimately philosophical, and he argued that the "remote cause" of the sectional crisis was the "false" and "pernicious" doctrine that "all men are born free and equal."*

. . . Now is the time to take the step, and bring about a result so devoutly to be wished. I have believed, from the beginning, that this was the only question sufficiently potent to dissolve the Union, and subvert our system of government; and that the sooner it was met and settled, the safer and better for all. I have never doubted but that, if permitted to progress beyond a certain point, its settlement would become impossible, and am under deep conviction that it is now rapidly approaching it—and that if it is ever to be averted, it must be done speedily. In uttering these opinions I look to the whole. If I speak earnestly, it is to save and protect all. As deep as is the stake of the South in the Union and our political institutions, it is not deeper than that of the North. We shall be as well prepared and as capable of meeting whatever may come, as you.

Now, let me say, Senators, if our Union and system of government are doomed to perish, and we to share the fate of so many great people who have gone before us, the historian, who, in some future day, may record the events ending in so calamitous a result, will devote his first chapter to the ordinance of 1787, lauded as it and its authors have been, as the first of that series which led to it. His next chapter will be devoted to the Missouri compromise, and the next to the present agitation. Whether there will be another beyond, I know not. It will depend on what we may do.

If he should possess a philosophical turn of mind, and be disposed to look to more remote and recondite causes, he will trace it to a proposition which originated in a hypothetical truism, but which, as now expressed and now understood, is the most false and dangerous of all political errors. The proposition to which I allude, has become an axiom in the minds of a vast majority on both sides of the Atlantic, and is repeated daily from tongue to tongue, as an established and incontrovertible truth; it is, that "all men are born free and equal." I am not afraid to attack error, however deeply it may be intrenched, or however widely extended, whenever it becomes my duty to do so, as I believe it to be on this subject and occasion.

Taking the proposition literally (it is in that sense it is understood), there is not a word of truth in it. It begins with "all men are born," which is utterly untrue. Men are not born. Infants are born. They grow to be men. And concludes with asserting that they are born "free and equal," which is not less false. They are not born free. While infants they are incapable of freedom, being destitute alike of the capacity of thinking and acting, without which there can be no freedom. Besides, they are necessarily born subject to their parents, and remain so among all people, savage and civilized, until the development of their intellect and physical capacity enables them to take care of themselves. They grow to all the freedom of which the condition in which they were born permits, by growing to be men. Nor is it less false that they are born "equal." They are not so in any sense in which it can be regarded; and thus, as I have asserted, there is not a word of truth in the whole proposition, as expressed and generally understood.

If we trace it back, we shall find the proposition differently expressed in the Declaration of Independence. That asserts that "all men are created equal." The form of expression, though less dangerous, is not less erroneous. All men are not created. According to the Bible, only two, a man and a woman, ever were, and of these one was pronounced subordinate to the other. All others have come into the world by being born, and in no sense, as I have shown, either free or equal. But this form of expression being less striking and popular, has given way to the present, and under the authority of a document put forth on so great an occasion, and leading to such important consequences, has spread far and wide, and fixed itself deeply in the public mind. It was inserted in our Declaration of Independence without any necessity. It made no necessary part of our justification in separating from the parent country, and declaring ourselves independent. Breach of our chartered privileges, and lawless encroachment on our acknowledged and well-established rights by the parent country, were the real causes, and of themselves sufficient, without resorting to any other, to justify the step. Nor had it any weight in constructing the governments which were substituted in the place of the colonial. They were formed of the old materials and on practical and well-established principles, borrowed for the most part from our own experience and that of the country from which we sprang.

If the proposition be traced still further back, it will be found to have been adopted from certain writers on government who had attained much celebrity in the early settlement of these States, and with whose writings all the prominent actors in our revolution were familiar. Among these, Locke and Sydney were prominent. But they expressed it very differently. According to their expression, "all men in the state of nature were free and equal." From this the others were derived; and it was this to which I referred when I called it a hypothetical truism. To understand why, will require some explanation.

Man, for the purpose of reasoning, may be regarded in three different states: in a state of individuality; that is, living by himself apart from the rest of his species. In the social; that is, living in society, associated with others of his species. And in the political; that is, being under government. We may reason as to what would be his rights and duties in either, without taking into consideration whether he could exist in it or not. It is certain, that in the first, the very supposition that he lived apart and separated from all others, would make him free and equal. No one in such a state could have the right to command or control another. Every man would be his own master, and might do just as he pleased. But it is equally clear, that man cannot exist in such a state; that he is by nature social, and that society is necessary, not only to the proper development of all his faculties, moral and intellectual, but to the very existence of his race. Such being the case, the state is a purely hypothetical one; and when we say all men are free and equal in it, we announce a mere hypothetical truism; that is, a truism resting on a mere supposition that cannot exist, and of course one of little or no practical value.

But to call it a state of nature was a great misnomer, and has led to dangerous errors; for that cannot justly be called a state of nature which is so opposed to the constitution of man as to be inconsistent with the existence of his race and the development of the high faculties, mental and moral, with which he is endowed by his Creator.

Nor is the social state of itself his natural state; for society can no more exist without government, in one form or another, than man without society. It is the political, then, which includes the social, that is his natural state. It is the one for which his Creator formed him, into which he is impelled irresistibly, and in which only his race can exist and all its faculties be fully developed.

Such being the case, it follows that any, the worst form of government, is better than anarchy; and that individual liberty, or freedom, must be subordinate to whatever power may be necessary to protect society against anarchy within or destruction from without; for the safety and well-being of society is as paramount to individual liberty, as the safety and well-being of the race is to that of individuals; and in the same proportion, the power necessary for the safety of society is paramount to individual liberty. On the contrary, government has no right to control individual liberty beyond what is necessary to the safety and well-being of society. Such is the boundary which separates the power of government and the liberty of the citizen or subject in the political state, which, as I have shown, is the natural state of man—the only one in which his race can exist, and the one in which he is born, lives, and dies.

It follows from all this that the quantum of power on the part of the government, and of liberty on that of individuals, instead of being equal in all cases, must necessarily be very unequal among different people, according to their different conditions. For just in proportion as a people are ignorant, stupid, debased, corrupt, exposed to violence within and danger from without, the power necessary for government to possess, in order to preserve society against anarchy and destruction becomes greater and greater, and individual liberty less and less, until the lowest condition is reached, when absolute and despotic power becomes necessary on the part of the government, and individual liberty extinct. So, on the contrary, just as a people rise in the scale of intelligence, virtue, and patriotism, and the more perfectly they become acquainted with the nature of government, the ends for which it was ordered, and how it ought to be administered, and the less the tendency to violence and disorder within, and danger from abroad, the power necessary for government becomes less and less, and individual liberty greater and greater. Instead, then, of all men having the same right to liberty and equality, as is claimed by those who hold that they are all born free and equal, liberty is the noble and highest reward bestowed on mental and moral development, combined with favorable circumstances. Instead, then, of liberty and equality being born with man; instead of all men and all classes and descriptions being equally entitled to them, they are high prizes to be won, and are in their most perfect state, not only the highest reward that can be bestowed on our race, but the most difficult to be won—and when won, the most difficult to be preserved.

They have been made vastly more so by the dangerous error I have attempted to expose, that all men are born free and equal, as if those high qualities belonged to man without effort to acquire them, and to all equally alike, regardless of their intellectual and moral condition. The attempt to carry into practice this, the most dangerous of all political error, and to bestow on all, without regard to their fitness either to acquire or maintain liberty, that unbounded and individual liberty supposed to belong to man in the hypothetical and misnamed state of nature, has done more to retard the cause of liberty and civilization, and is doing more at present, than all other causes combined. While it is powerful to pull down governments, it is still more powerful to prevent their construction on proper principles. It is the leading cause among those which have placed Europe in its present anarchical condition, and which mainly stands in the way of reconstructing good governments in the place of those which have been overthrown, threatening thereby the quarter of the globe most advanced in progress and civilization with hopeless anarchy, to be followed by military despotism. Nor are we exempt from its disorganizing effects. We now begin to experience the danger of admitting so great an error to have a place in the declaration of our independence. For a long time it lay dormant; but in the process of time it began to germinate, and produce its poisonous fruits. It had strong hold on the mind of Mr. Jefferson, the author of that document, which caused him to take an utterly false view of the subordinate relation of the black to the white race in the South; and to hold, in consequence, that the former, though utterly unqualified to possess liberty, were as fully entitled to both liberty and equality as the latter; and that to deprive them of it was unjust and immoral. To this error, his proposition to exclude slavery from the territory northwest of the Ohio may be traced, and to that the ordinance of '87, and through it the deep and dangerous agitation which now threatens to ingulf, and will certainly ingulf, if not speedily settled, our political institutions, and involve the country in countless woes.

17

What to a Slave is the Fourth of July?

Frederick Douglass, 1852

> *After escaping the life of slavery he had been born into, Frederick Douglass (1818–1895) became a prominent abolitionist orator, newspaper editor, and diplomat. Douglass delivered the following oration to the Rochester Ladies' Anti-Slavery Society on the Fourth of July, 1852.*

Fellow citizens, pardon me, allow me to ask, why am I called upon to speak here today? What have I, or those I represent, to do with your national independence? Are the great principles of political freedom and natural justice, embodied in that Declaration of Independence, extended to us? And am I, therefore, called upon to bring our humble offering to the national altar, and to confess the benefits and express devout gratitude for the blessings resulting from your independence to us?

Would to God, both for your sakes and ours, that an affirmative answer could be truthfully returned to these questions! Then would my task be light, and my burden easy and delightful. For who is there so cold, that a nation's sympathy could not warm him? Who so obdurate and dead to the claims of gratitude, that would not thankfully acknowledge such priceless benefits? Who so stolid and selfish, that would not give his voice to swell the hallelujahs of a nation's jubilee, when the chains of servitude had been torn from his limbs? I am not that man. In a case like that, the dumb might eloquently speak, and the "lame man leap as an hart."

But such is not the state of the case. I say it with a sad sense of the disparity between us. I am not included within the pale of glorious anniversary! Your high independence only reveals the immeasurable distance between us. The blessings in which you, this day, rejoice, are not enjoyed in common. The rich inheritance of justice, liberty, prosperity and independence, bequeathed by your fathers, is shared by you, not by me. The sunlight that brought light and healing to you, has brought stripes and death to me.

This Fourth July is yours, not mine. You may rejoice, I must mourn. To drag a man in fetters into the grand illuminated temple of liberty, and call upon him to join you in joyous anthems, were inhuman mockery and sacrilegious irony. Do you mean, citizens, to mock me, by asking me to speak today?

FELLOW CITIZENS, above your national, tumultuous joy, I hear the mournful wail of millions!--whose chains, heavy and grievous yesterday, are, today, rendered more intolerable by the jubilee shouts that reach them. If I do forget, if I do not faithfully remember those bleeding children of sorrow this day, "may my right hand forget her cunning, and may my tongue cleave to the roof of my mouth!" To forget them, to pass lightly over their wrongs, and to chime in with the popular theme, would be treason most scandalous and shocking, and would make me a reproach before God and the world.

My subject, then, fellow citizens, is American slavery. I shall see this day and its popular characteristics from the slave's point of view. Standing there, identified with the American bondman, making his wrongs mine, I do not hesitate to declare, with all my soul, that the character and conduct of this nation never looked blacker to me than on this 4th of July!

Whether we turn to the declarations of the past, or to the professions of the present, the conduct of the nation seems equally hideous and revolting. America is false to the past, false to the present, and solemnly binds herself to be false to the future. Standing with God and the crushed and bleeding slave on this occasion, I will, in the name of humanity which is outraged, in the name of liberty which is fettered, in the name of the Constitution and Bible which are disregarded and trampled upon, dare to call in question and to denounce, with all the emphasis I can command, everything that serves to perpetuate slavery--the great sin and shame of America!

"I will not equivocate; I will not excuse"; I will use the severest language I can command; and yet not one word shall escape me that any man, whose judgement is not blinded by prejudice, or who is not at heart a slaveholder, shall not confess to be right and just.

But I fancy I hear some of my audience say, it is just in this circumstance that you and your brother abolitionists fail to make a favorable impression on the public mind. Would you argue more, and denounce less, would you persuade more, and rebuke less, your cause would be much more likely to succeed.

But, I submit, where all is plain there is nothing to be argued. What point in the anti-slavery creed would you have me argue? On what branch of the subject do the people of this country need light? Must I undertake to prove that the slave is a man? That point is conceded already. Nobody doubts it. The slaveholders themselves acknowledge it in the enactment of laws for their government. They acknowledge it when they punish disobedience on the part of the slave. There are 72 crimes in the state of Virginia, which, if committed by a black man (no matter how ignorant he be), subject him to the punishment of death; while only two of the same crimes will subject a white man to the like punishment.

What is this but the acknowledgment that the slave is a moral, intellectual and responsible being? The manhood of the slave is conceded. It is admitted in the fact that Southern statute books are covered with enactments forbidding, under severe fines and penalties, the teaching of the slave to read or to write.

When you can point to any such laws, in reference to the beasts of the field, then I may consent to argue the manhood of the slave. When the dogs in your streets, when the fowls of the air, when the cattle on your hills, when the fish of the sea, and the reptiles that crawl, shall be unable to distinguish the slave from a brute, then will I argue with you that the slave is a man!

For the present, it is enough to affirm the equal manhood of the Negro race. Is it not astonishing that, while we are plowing, planting, and reaping, using all kinds of mechanical tools, erecting houses, constructing bridges, building ships, working in metals of brass, iron, copper, silver and gold; that, while we are reading, writing and ciphering, acting as clerks, merchants and secretaries, having among us lawyers, doctors, ministers, poets, authors, editors, orators and teachers; that, while we are engaged in all manner of enterprises common to other men, digging gold in California, capturing the whale in the Pacific, feeding sheep and cattle on the hillside, living, moving, acting, thinking, planning, living in families as husbands, wives and children, and, above all, confessing and worshipping the Christian's God, and looking hopefully for life and immortality beyond the grave, we are called upon to prove that we are men!

Would you have me argue that man is entitled to liberty? That he is the rightful owner of his own body? You have already declared it. Must I argue the wrongfulness of slavery? . . . To do so, would be to make myself ridiculous, and to offer an insult to your understanding. There is not a man beneath the canopy of heaven who does not know that slavery is wrong for him.

What, am I to argue that it is wrong to make men brutes, to rob them of their liberty, to work them without wages, to keep them ignorant of their relations to their fellow men, to beat them with sticks, to flay their flesh with the lash, to load their limbs with irons, to hunt them with dogs, to sell them at auction, to sunder their families, to knock out their teeth, to burn their flesh, to starve them into obedience and submission to their masters?

Must I argue that a system thus marked with blood, and stained with pollution, is wrong? No! I will not. I have better employments for my time and strength than such arguments would imply.

What, then, remains to be argued? Is it that slavery is not divine; that God did not establish it; that our doctors of divinity are mistaken? There is blasphemy in the thought. That which is inhuman cannot be divine! Who can reason on such a proposition? They that can, may; I cannot. The time for such argument is passed.

At a time like this, scorching irony, not convincing argument, is needed. Oh! Had I the ability, and could reach the nation's ear, I would today pour out a fiery stream of biting ridicule, blasting reproach, withering sarcasm, and stern rebuke. For it is not light that is needed, but fire; it is not the gentle shower, but thunder. We need the storm, the whirlwind, and the earthquake. The feeling of the nation must be quickened; the conscience of the nation must be roused; the propriety of the nation must be startled; the hypocrisy of the nation must be exposed; and its crimes against God and man must be proclaimed and denounced.

WHAT TO the American slave is your 4th of July? I answer: a day that reveals to him, more than all other days in the year, the gross injustice and cruelty to which he is the constant victim. To him, your celebration is a sham; your boasted liberty, an unholy license; your national greatness, swelling vanity; your sounds of rejoicing are empty and heartless; your denunciations of tyrants, brass fronted impudence; your shouts of liberty and equality, hollow mockery; your prayers and hymns, your sermons and thanksgivings, with all your religious parade and solemnity, are, to him, mere bombast, fraud, deception, impiety, and hypocrisy--a thin veil to cover up crimes which would disgrace a nation of savages. There is not a nation on the earth guilty of practices more shocking and bloody than are the people of the United States, at this very hour.

Go where you may, search where you will, roam through all the monarchies and despotisms of the Old World, travel through South America, search out every abuse, and when you have found the last, lay your facts by the side of the everyday practices of this nation, and you will say with me that, for revolting barbarity and shameless hypocrisy, America reigns without a rival.

Fellow citizens, the murderous traffic [the slave trade] is today in active operation in this boasted republic. In the solitude of my spirit, I see clouds of dust raised on the highways of the South; I see the bleeding footsteps; I hear the doleful wail of fettered humanity, on the way to the slave markets, where the victims are to be sold like horses, sheep, and swine, knocked off to the highest bidder. There I see the tenderest ties ruthlessly broken, to gratify the lust, caprice and rapacity of the buyers and sellers of men. My soul sickens at the sight.

Fellow citizens! The existence of slavery in this country brands your republicanism as a sham, your humanity as a base pretence, and your Christianity as a lie. It destroys your moral power abroad; it corrupts your politicians at home. It saps the foundation of religion; it makes your name a hissing, and a byword to a mocking earth. It is the antagonistic force in your government, the only thing that seriously disturbs and endangers your Union. It fetters your progress; it is the enemy of improvement, the deadly foe of education; it fosters pride; it breeds insolence; it promotes vice; it shelters crime; it is a curse to the earth that supports it; and yet, you cling to it, as if it were the sheet anchor of all your hopes

Oh be warned! Be warned! A horrible reptile is coiled up in your nation's bosom; the venomous creature is nursing at the tender breast of your youthful republic; for the love of God, tear away, and fling from you the hideous monster, and let the weight of twenty millions crush and destroy it forever!

18

Party Platform

Republican National Convention, 1856

> *In 1854, Congress passed the Kansas–Nebraska Act, which allowed settlers in the territories of Kansas and Nebraska to determine whether or not to allow slavery within their borders. The Act repealed certain aspects of the Missouri Compromise (1820), which had "forever prohibited" slavery in the territories north and west of Missouri. The Republican Party platform of 1856 was written in opposition to the Kansas-Nebraska Act and had, as its express purpose, the "maintenance of the principles promulgated in the Declaration of Independence."*

This Convention of Delegates, assembled in pursuance of a call addressed to the people of the United States, without regard to past political differences or divisions, who are opposed to the repeal of the Missouri Compromise; to the policy of the present Administration; to the extension of Slavery into Free Territory; in favor of the admission of Kansas as a Free State; of restoring the action of the Federal Government to the principles of Washington and Jefferson; and for the purpose of presenting candidates for the offices of President and Vice-President, do

Resolved: That the maintenance of the principles promulgated in the Declaration of Independence, and embodied in the Federal Constitution are essential to the preservation of our Republican institutions, and that the Federal Constitution, the rights of the States, and the union of the States, must and shall be preserved.

Resolved: That, with our Republican fathers, we hold it to be a self-evident truth, that all men are endowed with the inalienable right to life, liberty, and the pursuit of happiness, and that the primary object and ulterior design of our Federal Government were to secure these rights to all persons under its exclusive jurisdiction; that, as our Republican fathers, when they had abolished Slavery in all our National Territory, ordained that no person shall be deprived of life, liberty, or property, without due process of law, it becomes our duty to maintain this provision of the Constitution against all attempts to violate it for the purpose of establishing Slavery in the Territories of the United States by positive legislation, prohibiting its existence or extension therein. That we deny the authority of Congress, of a Territorial Legislation, of any individual, or association of individuals, to give legal existence to Slavery in any Territory of the United States, while the present Constitution shall be maintained.

Resolved: That the Constitution confers upon Congress sovereign powers over the Territories of the United States for their government; and that in the exercise of this power, it is both the right and the imperative duty of Congress to prohibit in the Territories those twin relics of barbarism—Polygamy, and Slavery.

Resolved: That while the Constitution of the United States was ordained and established by the people, in order to "form a more perfect union, establish justice, insure domestic tranquility, provide for the common defense, promote the general welfare, and secure the blessings of liberty," and contain ample provision for the protection of the life, liberty, and property of every citizen, the dearest Constitutional rights of the people of Kansas have been fraudulently and violently taken from them.

19

The *Dred Scott* Decision

Chief Justice Roger Taney, 1857

> In Dred Scott v. Sandford (1857), the Supreme Court ruled in part that African slaves and their descendants were not, and could never become, citizens of the United States. The following excerpt is from the opinion of Chief Justice Roger Taney, who asserted that Africans were "not intended to be included" as part of the people for whom the Declaration of Independence and the Constitution were written.

... The question is simply this: Can a negro, whose ancestors were imported into this country, and sold as slaves, become a member of the political community formed and brought into existence by the Constitution of the United States, and as such become entitled to all the rights, and privileges, and immunities, guaranteed by that instrument to the citizen? One of which rights is the privilege of suing in a court of the United States in the cases specified in the Constitution.

It will be observed, that the plea applies to that class of persons only whose ancestors were negroes of the African race, and imported into this country, and sold and held as slaves. The only matter in issue before the court, therefore, is, whether the descendants of such slaves, when they shall be emancipated, or who are born of parents who had become free before their birth, are citizens of a State, in the sense in which the word citizen is used in the Constitution of the United States. And this being the only matter in dispute on the pleadings, the court must be understood as speaking in this opinion of that class only, that is, of those persons who are the descendants of Africans who were imported into this country, and sold as slaves . . .

The words 'people of the United States' and 'citizens' are synonymous terms, and mean the same thing. They both describe the political body who, according to our republican institutions, form the sovereignty, and who hold the power and conduct the Government through their representatives. They are what we familiarly call the 'sovereign people,' and every citizen is one of this people and a constituent member of this sovereignty. The question before us is, whether the class of persons described in the plea in abatement compose a portion of this people, and are constituent members of this sovereignty? We think they are not, and that they are not included, and were not intended to be included, under the word 'citizens' in the Constitution, and can therefore claim none of the rights and privileges which that instrument provides for and secures to citizens of the United States. On the contrary, they were at that time considered as a subordinate and inferior class of beings, who had been subjugated by the dominant race, and, whether emancipated or not, yet remained subject to their authority, and had no rights or privileges but such as those who held the power and the Government might choose to grant them.

It is not the province of the court to decide upon the justice or injustice, the policy or impolicy, of these laws. The decision of that question belonged to the political or law-making power; to those who formed the sovereignty and framed the Constitution. The duty of the court is, to interpret the instrument they have framed, with the best lights we can obtain on the subject, and to administer it as we find it, according to its true intent and meaning when it was adopted.

In discussing this question, we must not confound the rights of citizenship which a State may confer within its own limits, and the rights of citizenship as a member of the Union. It does not by any means follow, because he has all the rights and privileges of a citizen of a State, that he must be a citizen of the United States. He may have all of the rights and privileges of the citizen of a State, and yet not be entitled to the rights and privileges of a citizen in any other State. For, previous to the adoption of the Constitution of the United States, every State had the undoubted right to confer on whomsoever it pleased the character of citizen, and to endow him with all its rights. But this character of course was confined to the boundaries of the State, and gave him no rights or privileges in other States beyond those secured to him by the laws of nations and the comity of States. Nor have the several States surrendered the power of conferring these rights and privileges by adopting the Constitution of the United States. Each State may still confer them upon an alien, or any one it thinks proper, or upon any class or description of persons; yet he would not be a citizen in the sense in which that word is used in the Constitution of the United States, nor entitled to sue as such in one of its courts, nor to the privileges and immunities of a citizen in the other States. The rights which he would acquire would be restricted to the State which gave them. The Constitution has conferred on Congress the right to establish an uniform rule of naturalization, and this right is evidently exclusive, and has always been held by this court to be so. Consequently, no State, since the adoption of the Constitution, can by naturalizing an alien invest him with the rights and privileges secured to a citizen of a State under the Federal Government, although, so far as the State alone was concerned, he would undoubtedly be entitled to the rights of a citizen, and clothed with all the rights and immunities which the Constitution and laws of the State attached to that character.

It is very clear, therefore, that no State can, by any act or law of its own, passed since the adoption of the Constitution, introduce a new member into the political community created by the Constitution of the United States. It cannot make him a member of this community by making him a member of its own. And for the same reason it cannot introduce any person, or description of persons, who were not intended to be embraced in this new political family, which the Constitution brought into existence, but were intended to be excluded from it.

The question then arises, whether the provisions of the Constitution, in relation to the personal rights and privileges to which the citizen of a State should be entitled, embraced the negro African race, at that time in this country, or who might afterwards be imported, who had then or should afterwards be made free in any State; and to put it in the power of a single State to make him a citizen of the United States, and endue him with the full rights of citizenship in every other State without their consent? Does the Constitution of the United States act upon him whenever he shall be made free under the laws of a State, and raised there to the rank of a citizen, and immediately clothe him with all the privileges of a citizen in every other State, and in its own courts?

The court think the affirmative of these propositions cannot be maintained. And if it cannot, the plaintiff in error could not be a citizen of the State of Missouri, within the meaning of the Constitution of the United States, and, consequently, was not entitled to sue in its courts.

It is true, every person, and every class and description of persons, who were at the time of the adoption of the Constitution recognised as citizens in the several States, became also citizens of this new political body; but none other; it was formed by them, and for them and their posterity, but for no one else. And the personal rights and privileges guarantied to citizens of this new sovereignty were intended to embrace those only who were then members of the several State communities, or who should afterwards by birthright or otherwise become members, according to the provisions of the Constitution and the principles on which it was founded. It was the union of those who were at that time members of distinct and separate political communities into one political family, whose power, for certain specified purposes, was to extend over the whole territory of the United States. And it gave to each citizen rights and privileges outside of his State which he did not before possess, and placed him in every other State upon a perfect equality with its own citizens as to rights of person and rights of property; it made him a citizen of the United States.

It becomes necessary, therefore, to determine who were citizens of the several States when the Constitution was adopted. And in order to do this, we must recur to the Governments and institutions of the thirteen colonies, when they separated from Great Britain and formed new sovereignties, and took their places in the family of independent nations. We must inquire who, at that time, were recognised as the people or citizens of a State, whose rights and liberties had been outraged by the English Government; and who declared their independence, and assumed the powers of Government to defend their rights by force of arms.

In the opinion of the court, the legislation and histories of the times, and the language used in the Declaration of Independence, show, that neither the class of persons who had been imported as slaves, nor their descendants, whether they had become free or not, were then acknowledged as a part of the people, nor intended to be included in the general words used in that memorable instrument.

It is difficult at this day to realize the state of public opinion in relation to that unfortunate race, which prevailed in the civilized and enlightened portions of the world at the time of the Declaration of Independence, and when the Constitution of the United States was framed and adopted. But the public history of every European nation displays it in a manner too plain to be mistaken.

They had for more than a century before been regarded as beings of an inferior order, and altogether unfit to associate with the white race, either in social or political relations; and so far inferior, that they had no rights which the white man was bound to respect; and that the negro might justly and lawfully be reduced to slavery for his benefit. He was bought and sold, and treated as an ordinary article of merchandise and traffic, whenever a profit could be made by it. This opinion was at that time fixed and universal in the civilized portion of the white race. It was regarded as an axiom in morals as well as in politics, which no one thought of disputing, or supposed to be open to dispute and men in every grade and position in society daily and habitually acted upon it in their private pursuits, as well as in matters of public concern, without doubting for a moment the correctness of this opinion . . .

20

Debate on the *Dred Scott* Decision

Abraham Lincoln and Stephen Douglas, 1858

In the Illinois Senate campaign of 1858, Abraham Lincoln and Stephen Douglas engaged in a series of public debates that centered on the Dred Scott *decision. In the following excerpt, taken from their first debate in Ottawa, Illinois, Lincoln and Douglas dispute the relevance of the Declaration of Independence to the problem of slavery and American government.*

MR. DOUGLAS' SPEECH

... We are told by Lincoln that he is utterly opposed to the Dred Scott decision, and will not submit to it, for the reason that he says it deprives the negro of the rights and privileges of citizenship. [Laughter and applause.] That is the first and main reason which he assigns for his warfare on the Supreme Court of the United States and its decision. I ask you, are you in favor of conferring upon the negro the rights and privileges of citizenship? ["No, no."] Do you desire to strike out of our State Constitution that clause which keeps slaves and free negroes out of the State, and allow the free negroes to flow in, ["Never,"] and cover your prairies with black settlements? Do you desire to turn this beautiful State into a free negro colony, ["No, no,"] in order that when Missouri abolishes slavery she can send one hundred thousand emancipated slaves into Illinois, to become citizens and voters, on an equality with yourselves? ["Never," "no."] If you desire negro citizenship, if you desire to allow them to come into the State and settle with the white man, if you desire them to vote on an equality with yourselves, and to make them eligible to office, to serve on juries, and to adjudge your rights, then support Mr. Lincoln and the Black Republican party, who are in favor of the citizenship of the negro. ["Never, never."] For one, I am opposed to negro citizenship in any and every form. [Cheers.] I believe this Government was made on the white basis. ["Good."] I believe it was made by white men for the benefit of white men and their posterity forever, and I am in favor of confining citizenship to white men, men of European birth and descent, instead of conferring it upon negroes, Indians, and other inferior races. ["Good for you." "Douglas forever."]

Mr. Lincoln, following the example and lead of all the little Abolition orators, who go around and lecture in the basements of schools and churches, reads from the Declaration of Independence, that all men were created equal, and then asks, how can you deprive a negro of that equality which God and the Declaration of Independence awards to him? He and they maintain that negro equality is guarantied by the laws of God, and that it is asserted in the Declaration of Independence. If they think so, of course they have a right to say so. and so vote. I do not question Mr. Lincoln's conscientious belief that the negro was made his equal, and hence is his brother, [Laughter,] but for my own part, I do not regard the negro as my equal, and positively deny that he is my brother or any kin to me whatever. ["Never." "Hit him again," and cheers.] Lincoln has evidently learned by heart Parson Lovejoy's catechism. [Laughter and applause.] He can repeat it as well as Farnsworth. and he is worthy of a medal from Father Giddings and Fred Douglass for his Abolitionism. [Laughter.] He holds that the negro was born his equal and yours, and that he was endowed with equality by the Almighty, and that no human law can deprive him of these rights which were guarantied to him by the Supreme ruler of the Universe. Now, I do not believe that the Almighty ever intended the negro to be the equal of the white man. ["Never, never."] If he did, he has been a long time demonstrating the fact. [Cheers.] For thousands of years the negro has been a race upon the earth, and during all that time, in all latitudes and climates, wherever he has wandered or been taken, he has been inferior to the race which he has there met. He belongs to an inferior race, and must always occupy an inferior position. ["Good," "that's so," &c.] I do not hold that because the negro is our inferior that, therefore, he ought to be a slave. By no means can such a conclusion be drawn from what I have said. On the contrary, I hold that humanity and Christianity both require that the negro shall have and enjoy every right, every privilege, and every immunity consistent with the safety of the society in which he lives. ["That's so."] On that point, I presume, there can be no diversity of opinion. You and I are bound to extend to our inferior and dependent beings every right, every privilege, every facility and immunity consistent with the public good. The question then arises, what rights and privileges are consistent with the public good? This is a question which each State and each Territory must decide for itself—Illinois has decided it for herself. We have provided that the negro shall not be a slave, and we have also provided that he shall not be a citizen, but protect him in his civil rights, in his life, his person and his property, only depriving him of all political rights whatsoever, and refusing to put him on an equality with the white man. ["Good."] That policy of Illinois is satisfactory to the Democratic party and to me, and if it were to the Republicans, there would then be no question upon the subject; but the Republicans say that he ought to be made a citizen, and when he becomes a citizen he becomes your equal, with all your rights and privileges. ["He never shall."] They assert the Dred Scott decision to be monstrous because it denies that the negro is or can be a citizen under the Constitution. Now, I hold that Illinois had a right to abolish and prohibit slavery as she did, and I hold that Kentucky has the same right to continue and protect slavery that Illinois had to abolish it. I hold that New York had as much right to abolish slavery as Virginia has to continue it, and that each and every State of this Union is a sovereign power, with the right to do as it pleases upon this question of slavery, and upon all its domestic institutions. Slavery is not the only question which comes up in this controversy. There is a far more important one to you, and that is, what shall be done with the free negro? We have settled the slavery question as far as we are concerned; we have prohibited it in Illinois forever, and in doing so, I think we have done wisely, and there is no man in the State who would be more strenuous in his opposition to the introduction of slavery than I would; [Cheers] but when we settled it for ourselves, we exhausted all our power over that subject. We have done our whole duty, and can do no more. We must leave each and every other State to decide for itself the same question. In relation to the policy to be pursued toward the free negroes, we have said that they shall not vote; whilst Maine, on the other hand, has said that they shall vote. Maine is a sovereign State, and has the power to regulate the qualifications of voters within her limits. I would never consent to confer the right of voting and of citizenship upon a negro, but still I am not going to quarrel with Maine for differing from me in opinion. Let Maine take care of her own negroes and fix the qualifications of her own voters to suit herself, without interfering with Illinois, and Illinois will not interfere with Maine. So with the State of New York. She allows the negro to vote provided he owns two hundred and fifty dollars' worth of property, but not otherwise. While I would not make any distinction whatever between a negro who held property and one who did not; yet if the sovereign State of New York chooses to make that distinction it is her business and not mine, and I will not quarrel with her for it. She can do as she pleases on this question if she minds her own business, and we will do the same thing. Now, my friends, if we will only act conscientiously and rigidly upon this great principle of popular sovereignty, which guaranties to each State and Territory the right to do as it pleases on all things, local and domestic, instead of Congress interfering, we will continue at peace one with another. Why should Illinois be at war with Missouri, or Kentucky with Ohio, or Virginia with New York, merely because their institutions differ? Our fathers intended that our institutions should differ. They knew that the North and the South, having different climates, productions and interests, required different institutions. This doctrine of Mr. Lincoln, of uniformity among the institutions of the different States, is a new doctrine, never dreamed of by Washington, Madison, or the framers of this Government. Mr. Lincoln and the Republican party set themselves up as wiser than these men who made this Government, which has flourished for seventy years under the principle of popular sovereignty, recognizing the right of each State to do as it pleased. Under that principle, we have grown from a nation of three or four millions to a nation of about thirty millions of people; we have crossed the Allegheny mountains and filled up the whole north-west, turning the prairie into a garden, and building up churches and schools, thus spreading civilization and Christianity where before there was nothing but savage barbarism. Under that principle we have become, from a feeble nation, the most powerful on the face of the earth, and if we only adhere to that principle, we can go forward increasing in territory, in power, in strength and in glory until the Republic of America shall be the North Star that shall guide the friends of freedom throughout the civilized world. ["Long may you live," and great applause.] And why can we not adhere to the great principle of self-government, upon which our institutions were originally based? ["We can."] I believe that this new doctrine preached by Mr. Lincoln and his party will dissolve the Union if it succeeds. They are trying to array all the Northern States in one body against the South, to excite a sectional war between the free States and the slave States, in order that the one or the other may be driven to the wall.

I am told that my time is out. Mr. Lincoln will now address you for an hour and a half, and I will then occupy an half hour in replying to him.

MR. LINCOLN'S REPLY

[Mr. Lincoln then came forward and was greeted with loud and protracted cheers from fully two-thirds of the audience. This was admitted by the Douglas men on the platform. It was some minutes before he could make himself heard, even by those on the stand. At last he said:]

I will say here, while upon this subject, that I have no purpose, directly or indirectly, to interfere with the institution of slavery in the States where it exists. I believe I have no lawful right to do so, and I have no inclination to do so. I have no purpose to introduce political and social equality between the white and the black races. There is a physical difference between the two, which, in my judgment, will probably forever forbid their living together upon the footing of perfect equality, and inasmuch as it becomes a necessity that there must be a difference, I, as well as Judge Douglas, am in favor of the race to which I belong having the superior position. I have never said anything to the contrary, but I hold that, notwithstanding all this, there is no reason in the world why the negro is not entitled to all the natural rights enumerated in the Declaration of Independence, the right to life, liberty, and the pursuit of happiness. [Loud cheers.] I hold that he is as much entitled to these as the white man. I agree with Judge Douglas he is not my equal in many respects—certainly not in color, perhaps not in moral or intellectual endowment. But in the right to eat the bread, without the leave of anybody else, which his own hand earns, *he is my equal and the equal of Judge Douglas, and the equal of every living man.* [Great applause.] . . .

Now, having spoken of the Dred Scott decision, one more word and I am done. Henry Clay, my beau ideal of a statesman, the man for whom I fought all my humble life—Henry Clay once said of a class of men who would repress all tendencies to liberty and ultimate emancipation, that they must, if they would do this, go back to the era of our Independence, and muzzle the cannon which thunders its annual joyous return; they must blow out the moral lights around us; they must penetrate the human soul, and eradicate there the love of liberty; and then, and not till then, could they perpetuate slavery in this country! [Loud cheers.] To my thinking, Judge Douglas is, by his example and vast influence, doing that very thing in this community, [Cheers,] when he says that the negro has nothing in the Declaration of Independence. Henry Clay plainly understood the contrary. Judge Douglas is going back to the era of our Revolution, and to the extent of his ability, muzzling the cannon which thunders its annual joyous return. When he invites any people, willing to have slavery, to establish it, he is blowing out the moral lights around us. [Cheers.] When he says he "cares not whether slavery is voted down or voted up"—that it is a sacred right of self-government—he is, in my judgment, penetrating the human soul and eradicating the light of reason and the love of liberty in this American people. [Enthusiastic and continued applause.] And now I will only say that when, by all these means and appliances, Judge Douglas shall succeed in bringing public sentiment to an exact accordance with his own views—when these vast assemblages shall echo back all these sentiments—when they shall come to repeat his views and to avow his principles, and to say all that he says on these mighty questions—then it needs only the formality of the second Dred Scott decision, which he endorses in advance, to make slavery alike lawful in all the States—old as well as new, North as well as South.

21

The Chief Cornerstone

Alexander Stephens, 1861

> In an extemporaneous speech delivered in Savannah in 1861, Vice President of the Confederate States of America Alexander Stephens criticized what he took to be the "prevailing ideas entertained by [Jefferson] and most of the leading statesmen" at the time of the American Founding: that the "enslavement of the African was in violation of the laws of nature." The Confederacy, Stephens argued, was "founded upon exactly the opposite idea . . . that the negro is not equal to the white man."

MR. STEPHENS ROSE AND SPOKE AS FOLLOWS:

. . . I was remarking, that we are passing through one of the greatest revolutions in the annals of the world. Seven States have within the last three months thrown off an old government and formed a new. This revolution has been signally marked, up to this time, by the fact of its having been accomplished without the loss of a single drop of blood. [Applause.]

This new constitution, or form of government, constitutes the subject to which your attention will be partly invited. In reference to it, I make this first general remark. It amply secures all our ancient rights, franchises, and liberties. All the great principles of Magna Charta are retained in it. No citizen is deprived of life, liberty, or property, but by the judgment of his peers under the laws of the land. The great principle of religious liberty, which was the honor and pride of the old constitution, is still maintained and secured. All the essentials of the old constitution, which have endeared it to the hearts of the American people, have been preserved and perpetuated. [Applause.] Some changes have been made. Of these I shall speak presently.

Some of these I should have preferred not to have seen made; but these, perhaps, meet the cordial approbation of a majority of this audience, if not an overwhelming majority of the people of the Confederacy. Of them, therefore, I will not speak. But other important changes do meet my cordial approbation. They form great improvements upon the old constitution. So, taking the whole new constitution, I have no hesitancy in giving it as my judgment that it is decidedly better than the old. [Applause.] . . .

But not to be tedious in enumerating the numerous changes for the better, allow me to allude to one other—though last, not least. The new constitution has put at rest, forever, all the agitating questions relating to our peculiar institution—African slavery as it exists amongst us—the proper status of the negro in our form of civilization. This was the immediate cause of the late rupture and present revolution. Jefferson in his forecast, had anticipated this, as the "rock upon which the old Union would split." He was right. What was conjecture with him, is now a realized fact. But whether he fully comprehended the great truth upon which that rock stood and stands, may be doubted. The prevailing ideas entertained by him and most of the leading statesmen at the time of the formation of the old constitution, were that the enslavement of the African was in violation of the laws of nature; that it was wrong in principle, socially, morally, and politically. It was an evil they knew not well how to deal with, but the general opinion of the men of that day was that, somehow or other in the order of Providence, the institution would be evanescent and pass away. This idea, though not incorporated in the constitution, was the prevailing idea at that time. The constitution, it is true, secured every essential guarantee to the institution while it should last, and hence no argument can be justly urged against the constitutional guarantees thus secured, because of the common sentiment of the day. Those ideas, however, were fundamentally wrong. They rested upon the assumption of the equality of races. This was an error. It was a sandy foundation, and the government built upon it fell when the "storm came and the wind blew."

Our new government is founded upon exactly the opposite idea; its foundations are laid, its corner-stone rests upon the great truth, that the negro is not equal to the white man; that slavery—subordination to the superior race—is his natural and normal condition. [Applause.] This, our new government, is the first, in the history of the world, based upon this great physical, philosophical, and moral truth. This truth has been slow in the process of its development, like all other truths in the various departments of science. It has been so even amongst us. Many who hear me, perhaps, can recollect well, that this truth was not generally admitted, even within their day. The errors of the past generation still clung to many as late as twenty years ago. Those at the North, who still cling to these errors, with a zeal above knowledge, we justly denominate fanatics. All fanaticism springs from an aberration of the mind—from a defect in reasoning. It is a species of insanity. One of the most striking characteristics of insanity, in many instances, is forming correct conclusions from fancied or erroneous premises; so with the antislavery fanatics; their conclusions are right if their premises were. They assume that the negro is equal, and hence conclude that he is entitled to equal privileges and rights with the white man. If their premises were correct, their conclusions would be logical and just—but their premise being wrong, their whole argument fails. I recollect once of having heard a gentleman from one of the northern States, of great power and ability, announce in the House of Representatives, with imposing effect, that we of the South would be compelled, ultimately, to yield upon this subject of slavery, that it was as impossible to war successfully against a principle in politics, as it was in physics or mechanics. That the principle would ultimately prevail. That we, in maintaining slavery as it exists with us, were warring against a principle, a principle founded in nature, the principle of the equality of men. The reply I made to him was, that upon his own grounds, we should, ultimately, succeed, and that he and his associates, in this crusade against our institutions, would ultimately fail. The truth announced, that it was as impossible to war successfully against a principle in politics as it was in physics and mechanics, I admitted; but told him that it was he, and those acting with him, who were warring against a principle. They were attempting to make things equal which the Creator had made unequal.

In the conflict thus far, success has been on our side, complete throughout the length and breadth of the Confederate States. It is upon this, as I have stated, our social fabric is firmly planted; and I cannot permit myself to doubt the ultimate success of a full recognition of this principle throughout the civilized and enlightened world.

As I have stated, the truth of this principle may be slow in development, as all truths are and ever have been, in the various branches of science. It was so with the principles announced by Galileo—it was so with Adam Smith and his principles of political economy. It was so with Harvey, and his theory of the circulation of the blood. It is stated that not a single one of the medical profession, living at the time of the announcement of the truths made by him, admitted them. Now, they are universally acknowledged. May we not, therefore, look with confidence to the ultimate universal acknowledgment of the truths upon which our system rests? It is the first government ever instituted upon the principles in strict conformity to nature, and the ordination of Providence, in furnishing the materials of human society. Many governments have been founded upon the principle of the subordination and serfdom of certain classes of the same race; such were and are in violation of the laws of nature. Our system commits no such violation of nature's laws. With us, all of the white race, however high or low, rich or poor, are equal in the eye of the law. Not so with the negro.

Subordination is his place. He, by nature, or by the curse against Canaan, is fitted for that condition which he occupies in our system. The architect, in the construction of buildings, lays the foundation with the proper material—the granite; then comes the brick or the marble. The substratum of our society is made of the material fitted by nature for it, and by experience we know that it is best, not only for the superior, but for the inferior race, that it should be so. It is, indeed, in conformity with the ordinance of the Creator. It is not for us to inquire into the wisdom of his ordinances, or to question them. For his own purposes, he has made one race to differ from another, as he has made "one star to differ from another star in glory."

The great objects of humanity are best attained when there is conformity to his laws and decrees, in the formation of governments as well as in all things else. Our confederacy is founded upon principles in strict conformity with these laws. This stone which was rejected by the first builders "is become the chief of the corner"—the real "corner-stone"—in our new edifice. [Applause.] . . .

22

Gettysburg Address

Abraham Lincoln, 1863

> On November 19, 1863, President Abraham Lincoln delivered the following address at the dedication of a national war cemetery in Gettysburg, Pennsylvania. In his brief remarks, Lincoln dated the birth of the nation to 1776 and offered his now familiar and celebrated interpretation of the Civil War as one fought so that the nation might "have a new birth of freedom."

Four score and seven years ago our fathers brought forth on this continent, a new nation, conceived in Liberty, and dedicated to the proposition that all men are created equal.

Now we are engaged in a great civil war, testing whether that nation, or any nation so conceived and so dedicated, can long endure. We are met on a great battlefield of that war. We have come to dedicate a portion of that field, as a final resting place for those who here gave their lives that that nation might live. It is altogether fitting and proper that we should do this.

But, in a larger sense, we can not dedicate—we can not consecrate—we can not hallow—this ground. The brave men, living and dead, who struggled here, have consecrated it, far above our poor power to add or detract. The world will little note, nor long remember what we say here, but it can never forget what they did here. It is for us the living, rather, to be dedicated here to the unfinished work which they who fought here have thus far so nobly advanced. It is rather for us to be here dedicated to the great task remaining before us—that from these honored dead we take increased devotion to that cause for which they gave the last full measure of devotion—that we here highly resolve that these dead shall not have died in vain—that this nation, under God, shall have a new birth of freedom—and that government of the people, by the people, for the people, shall not perish from the earth.

23

Reconstructing America

United States Congress, 1864–1870

> *After the Civil War, Congress amended the federal Constitution to, among other things, abolish slavery, grant birth citizenship, and ensure that states afford all persons the equal protection of the laws. The following excerpts are drawn from Reconstruction Era congressional debates on fundamental constitutional questions involving slavery, liberty, and civil rights.*

SLAVERY

Rep. James Wilson (R-IA):
Let us not overlook that portion of this well-expressed and better-bestowed praise which rests upon the fact that the glorious work of the people was for "the sake of all mankind." Let it bring afresh to our minds that important question propounded by Jefferson:

"Can the liberties of a nation be thought secure when we have removed their only firm basis, a conviction in the minds of the people that these liberties are the gift of God: that they are not to be violated but with His wrath?"

Has not slavery denied that this great work of the people was intended for the "safety of all mankind," and brought upon us the just chastisement of God, who intended "these liberties" for all of His creatures? What are the thunders of this war but the voice of God calling upon this nation to return from the evil paths, made rough by errors and misfortunes, blunders and crimes, made slippery by the warm, smoking blood of our brothers and friends, to the grand highway of national thrift, prosperity, happiness, glory and peace, in which He planted the feet of the fathers? Cannot we hear amid the wild rushing roar of this war storm the voice of Him who rides upon the winds and rules the tempest saying unto us, "You cannot have peace until you secure liberty to all who are subject to your laws?" Sir, this declaration must be heeded. It has been whispered into the ears of this nation since first we pronounced life, liberty, and the pursuit of happiness to be the inalienable rights of all men, and now it rolls in upon us like the voice of the ocean, thundering peace or war to our election. Which shall we elect? Shall it be peace? How can it be peace while liberty and slavery dwell together in our midst? These are enemies. These are ideas which cannot dwell together in harmony. How can we have peace? Let slavery die. Let its death be written in our Constitution. Let the Constitution "proclaim liberty throughout the land to all the inhabitants thereof." This is the way to peace—firm, enduring peace, embracing all mankind, and reaching to the most distant generations. In this way only can we secure liberty to ourselves and our posterity . . .

The great rights here enumerated were regarded by the people as too sacred and too essential to the preservation of their liberties to be trusted with no firmer defense than the rule that "Congress can exercise no power which is not delegated to it." Around this negative protection was erected the positive barrier of absolute prohibition. Freedom of speech and press, and the right of assemblage for the purpose of petition belong to every American citizen, high or low, rich or poor, wherever he may be within the jurisdiction of the United States. With these rights no State may interfere without breach of the bond which holds the Union together. How have these rights essential to liberty been respected in those sections of the Union where slavery held the reins of local authority and directed the thoughts, prejudices, and passions of the people? The bitter, cruel, relentless persecutions of the Methodists in the South, almost as void of pity as those which were visited upon the Huguenots in France, tell how utterly slavery disregards the right to a free exercise of religion. No religion which recognizes God's eternal attribute of justice and breathes that spirit of love which applies to all men the sublime commandment, "Whatsoever ye would that men should do unto you, do ye even so to them," can ever be allowed free exercise where slavery curses men and defies God. No religious denomination can flourish or even be tolerated where slavery rules without surrendering the choicest jewels of its faith into the keeping of that infidel power which withholds the Bible from the poor. Religion, "consisting in the performance of all known duties to God and our fellow-men," never has been and never will be allowed free exercise in any community where slavery dwarfs the consciences of men. The Constitution may declare the right, but slavery ever will, as it ever has, trample upon the Constitution and prevent the enjoyment of the right.

How much better has free discussion fared at the hands of the black censor who guards the interests of slavery against the expression of the thoughts of freemen? On what rood of this Republic cursed by slavery have men been free to declare their approval of the divine doctrines of the Declaration of Independence? Where, except in the free States of this Union, have the nation's toiling millions been permitted to assert their great protective doctrines, "The laborer is worthy of his hire?" What member of our great free labor force, North or South, could stand upon the presence of the despotism which owns men and combat the atrocious assertion that "Slavery is the natural and normal condition of the laboring man, whether white or black, with the noble declaration that "Labor being the sure foundation of the nation's prosperity should be performed by free men, for they alone have an interest in the preservation of free government," with any assurance that his life would not be exacted as the price of his temerity? . . .

An equal and exact observance of the constitutional rights of each and every citizen, in each and every State, is the end to which we should cause the lessons of this war to carry us. Whatever stands between us and the accomplishment of this great end should be removed. Can we reach this end and save slavery? Can we reconcile the antagonisms which have produced this war? Can we mix the oil and water of despotism and republicanism? Can we harmonize the contending elements of absolutism and free government? No, sir; it is not given to human power to accomplish these results. What, then, shall we do? Abolish slavery. How? By amending our national Constitution.. Why? Because slavery is incompatible with free government. Peace, prosperity, national harmony, progress, civilization, Christianity, all admonish us that our only safety lies in universal freedom.

LIBERTY

Rep. Ignatius Donnelly (R-MN):

Slavery consists in a deprivation of natural rights. A man may be a slave for a term of years as fully as though he were held for life; he may be a slave when deprived of a portion of the wages of his labor as fully as if deprived of all; he may be held down by unjust laws to a degraded and defenseless condition as fully as though his wrists were manacled; he may be oppressed by a convocation of masters called a Legislature as fully as by a single master. In short, he who is not entirely free is necessarily a slave.

What has the South done for the black man since the close of the rebellion?

Let us examine the black codes of the different States adopted since that time.

In South Carolina it is provided that all male negroes between two and twenty, and all females between two and eighteen, shall be bound out to some "master." The adult negro is compelled to enter into contract with a master, and the district judge, not the laborer, is to fix the value of the labor. If he thinks the compensation too small and will not work, he is vagrant, and can be hired out for a term of service at a rate again to be fixed by the judge. If a hired negro leaves his employer he forfeits his wages for the whole year.

The black code of Mississippi provides that no negro shall own or hire lands in the State; that he shall not sue nor testify in court against a white man; that he must be employed by a master before the second Monday in January, or he will be bound out—in other words, sold into slavery; that if he runs away the master may recover him and deduct the expenses out of his wages; and that if another man employs him he will be liable to an action for the damages . . .

For one, with the help of Almighty God, I shall never consent to such cruel injustice. Having voted to give the negro liberty, I shall vote to give him all things essential to liberty.

If degradation and oppression have, as it is alleged, unfitted him for freedom, surely continued degradation and oppression will not prepare him for it. If he is not to remain a brute you must give him that which will make him a man—opportunity. If he is, as it is claimed, an inferior being and unable to compete with the white man on terms of equality, surely you will not add to the injustice of nature by casting him beneath the feet of the white man. With what face can you reproach him with his degradation at the very moment you are striving to further degrade him? If he is, as you say, not fit to vote, give him a chance; let him make himself an independent laborer like yourself; let him own his own homestead; let the courts of justice be opened to him; and let his intellect, darkened by centuries of neglect, be illuminated by all the glorious lights of education. If after all this he proves himself an unworthy savage and brutal wretch, condemn him, but not till then.

CIVIL RIGHTS

Rep. John Bingham (R-MI):

What are civil rights? . . . I respectfully submit . . . that by all authority the term "civil rights" as used in this [civil rights] bill does include and embrace every right that pertains to the citizen as such . . .

I submit that the term civil rights includes every right that pertains to the citizen under the Constitution, laws, and Government of this country. The term "citizen" has had a definite meaning among publicists ever since the days of Aristotle. He interpreted and rendered that term to signify a person who was a partner in the government of the country. Under the Constitution of the United States every natural-born citizen of the Republic is, in some sense, a partner in the Government, although he may take no active part in it.

Sen. Lyman Trumbull (R-IL):
But, sir, what rights do citizens of the United States have? To be a citizen of the United States carries with it some rights; and what are they? They are those inherent, fundamental rights which belong to free citizens or free men in all countries, such as the rights enumerated in this bill, and they belong to them in all the States of the Union . . . These rights belonging to the citizen, and known as natural rights, are defined by Blackstone in his definition of civil liberty to be:

"No other than a natural liberty, so far restrained by human laws and no further, as is necessary and expedient to the general advantage of the public. In this definition of civil liberty it ought to be understood, or rather expressed, that the restraints introduced by the law should be *equal to all*, or as much so as the nature of things will admit."

"The equality of rights is the basis of a commonwealth" is said in a note to Kent, and Kent himself, in speaking of these rights, says:

"The absolute rights of individuals may be resolved into the right of personal security, the right of personal liberty, and the right to acquire and enjoy property. These rights have been justly considered, and frequently declared, by the people of this country to be natural, inherent, and inalienable."

What are they? "The right of personal security, the right of personal liberty, and the right to acquire and enjoy property;" and these are declared to be inalienable rights, belonging to every citizen of the United States, as such, no matter where he may be.

Sen. Jacob Howard (R-MI):
It would be a curious question to solve what are the privileges and immunities of citizens of each of the States in the several States . . . we may gather some intimation of what probably will be the opinion of the judiciary by referring to a case adjudged many years ago . . . It is the case of Corfield v. Coryell, found in 4 Washington's Circuit Court Reports, page 380. Judge Washington says . . .

"The inquiry is, what are the privileges and immunities of citizens in the several States? We feel no hesitation in confining these expressions to those privileges and immunities which are in their nature fundamental, which belong of right to the citizens of all free Governments, and which have at all times been enjoyed by the citizens of the several States which compose this Union from the time of their becoming free, independent, and sovereign. What these fundamental principles are it would, perhaps be more tedious than difficult to enumerate. They may, however, be all comprehended under the following general heads: protection by the Government, the enjoyment of life and liberty, with the right to acquire and possess property of every kind, and to pursue and obtain happiness and safety, subject nevertheless to such restraints as the Government may justly prescribe for the general good of the whole. The right of a citizen of one State to pass through or to reside in any other State, for purposes of trade, agriculture, professional pursuits, or otherwise; to claim the benefit of the writ of habeas corpus; to institute and maintain actions of any kind in the courts of the State; to take, hold, and dispose of property, either real or personal, and an exemption from higher taxes or impositions than are paid by other citizens of the State, may be mentioned as some of the particularly embraced by the general description of privileges deemed to be fundamental, to which may be added the elective franchise, as regulated and established by the laws or constitution of the state in which it is to be exercised. These, and many other which might be mentioned, are, strictly speaking, privileges and immunities, and the enjoyment of them by the citizens of each State in every other State was manifestly calculated (to use the expressions of the preamble of the corresponding provision in the old Articles of Confederation) the better to secure and perpetuate mutual friendship and intercourse among the people of the different States of the Union."

Such is the character of the privileges and immunities spoken of in the second section of the fourth article of the Constitution. To these privileges and immunities, whatever they may be—for they are not and cannot be fully defined in their entire extent and precise nature—to these should be added the personal rights guarantied and secured by the first eight amendments of the Constitution; such as the freedom of speech and of the press; the right of the people peaceably to assemble and petition the Government for a redress of grievances, a right appertaining to each and all the people; the right to keep and to bear arms; the right to be exempted from the quartering of soldiers in a house without the consent of the owner; the right to be exempt from unreasonable searches and seizures, and from any search or seizure except by virtue of a warrant issued upon a formal oath or affidavit; the right of an accused person to be informed of the nature of the accusation against him, and his right to be tried by an impartial jury of the vicinage; and also the right to be secure against excessive bail and against cruel and unusual punishments.

III
THE DECLARATION IN THE MODERN WORLD

24

Seneca Falls Declaration

Elizabeth Cady Stanton and Lucretia Mott, 1848

> Elizabeth Cady Stanton (1815–1902) and Lucretia Mott (1793–1880) presented the following declaration at the first women's rights convention held in Seneca Falls, New York in 1848. Modeled after the U.S. Declaration of Independence, the Seneca Falls Declaration framed the issue of women's rights in terms of natural equality and contained a detailed list of "repeated injuries and usurpations on the part of man toward woman."

When, in the course of human events, it becomes necessary for one portion of the family of man to assume among the people of the earth a position different from that which they have hitherto occupied, but one to which the laws of nature and of nature's God entitle them, a decent respect to the opinions of mankind requires that they should declare the causes that impel them to such a course.

We hold these truths to be self-evident: that all men and women are created equal; that they are endowed by their Creator with certain inalienable rights; that among these are life, liberty, and the pursuit of happiness; that to secure these rights governments are instituted, deriving their just powers from the consent of the governed. Whenever any form of government becomes destructive of these ends, it is the right of those who suffer from it to refuse allegiance to it, and to insist upon the institution of a new government, laying its foundation on such principles, and organizing its powers in such form, as to them shall seem most likely to effect their safety and happiness. Prudence, indeed, will dictate that governments long established should not be changed for light and transient causes; and accordingly all experience hath shown that mankind are more disposed to suffer, while evils are sufferable, than to right themselves by abolishing the forms to which they were accustomed. But when a long train of abuses and usurpations, pursuing invariably the same object, evinces a design to reduce them under absolute despotism, it is their duty to throw off such government, and to provide new guards for their future security. Such has been the patient sufferance of the women under this government, and such is now the necessity which constrains them to demand the equal station to which they are entitled.

The history of mankind is a history of repeated injuries and usurpations on the part of man toward woman, having in direct object the establishment of an absolute tyranny over her. To prove this, let facts be submitted to a candid world.

He has never permitted her to exercise her inalienable right to the elective franchise.

He has compelled her to submit to laws, in the formation of which she had no voice.

He has withheld from her rights which are given to the most ignorant and degraded men—both natives and foreigners.

Having deprived her of this first right of a citizen, the elective franchise, thereby leaving her without representation in the halls of legislation, he has oppressed her on all sides.

He has made her, if married, in the eye of the law, civilly dead.

He has taken from her all right in property, even to the wages she earns.

He has made her, morally, an irresponsible being, as she can commit many crimes with impunity, provided they be done in the presence of her husband. In the covenant of marriage, she is compelled to promise obedience to her husband, he becoming, to all intents and purposes, her master—the law giving him power to deprive her of her liberty, and to administer chastisement.

He has so framed the laws of divorce, as to what shall be the proper causes, and in case of separation, to whom the guardianship of the children shall be given, as to be wholly regardless of the happiness of women—the law, in all cases, going upon a false supposition of the supremacy of man, and giving all power into his hands.

After depriving her of all rights as a married woman, if single, and the owner of property, he has taxed her to support a government which recognizes her only when her property can be made profitable to it.

He has monopolized nearly all the profitable employments, and from those she is permitted to follow, she receives but a scanty remuneration. He closes against her all the avenues to wealth and distinction which he considers most honorable to himself. As a teacher of theology, medicine, or law, she is not known.

He has denied her the facilities for obtaining a thorough education, all colleges being closed against her.

He allows her in Church, as well as State, but a subordinate position, claiming Apostolic authority for her exclusion from the ministry, and, with some exceptions, from any public participation in the affairs of the Church.

He has created a false public sentiment by giving to the world a different code of morals for men and women, by which moral delinquencies which exclude women from society, are not only tolerated, but deemed of little account in man.

He has usurped the prerogative of Jehovah himself, claiming it as his right to assign for her a sphere of action, when that belongs to her conscience and to her God.

He has endeavored, in every way that he could, to destroy her confidence in her own powers, to lessen her self-respect, and to make her willing to lead a dependent and abject life.

Now, in view of this entire disfranchisement of one-half the people of this country, their social and religious degradation—in view of the unjust laws above mentioned, and because women do feel themselves aggrieved, oppressed, and fraudulently deprived of their most sacred rights, we insist that they have immediate admission to all the rights and privileges which belong to them as citizens of the United States.

In entering upon the great work before us, we anticipate no small amount of misconception, misrepresentation, and ridicule; but we shall use every instrumentality within our power to effect our object. We shall employ agents, circulate tracts, petition the State and National legislatures, and endeavor to enlist the pulpit and the press in our behalf. We hope this Convention will be followed by a series of Conventions embracing every part of the country.

The following resolutions were discussed by Lucretia Mott, Thomas and Mary Ann McClintock, Amy Post, Catherine A. F. Stebbins, and others, and were adopted:

WHEREAS, The great precept of nature is conceded to be, that "man shall pursue his own true and substantial happiness." Blackstone in his Commentaries remarks, that this law of Nature being coeval with mankind, and dictated by God himself, is of course superior in obligation to any other. It is binding over all the globe, in all countries and at all times no human laws are of any validity if contrary to this, and such of them as are valid, derive all their force, and all their validity, and all their authority, immediately and immediately, from this original; therefore,

Resolved, That such laws as conflict, in any way, with the true and substantial happiness of woman, are contrary to the great precept of Nature and of no validity, for this is "superior in obligation to any other."

Resolved, That all laws which prevent woman from occupying such a station in society as her conscience shall dictate, or which place her in a position inferior to that of man. are contrary to the great precept of Nature, and therefore of no force or authority.

Resolved, That woman is man's equal—was intended to be so by the Creator, and the highest good of the race demands that she should be recognized as such.

Resolved, That the women of this country ought to be enlightened in regard to the laws under which they live, that they may no longer publish their degradation by declaring themselves satisfied with their present position, nor their ignorance, by asserting that they have all the rights they want.

Resolved, That inasmuch as man, while claiming for himself intellectual superiority, does accord to woman moral superiority, it is pre-eminently his duty to encourage her to speak and teach as she has opportunity, in all religious assemblies.

Resolved, That the same amount of virtue, delicacy, and refinement of behavior that is required of woman in the social state, should also be required of man, and the same transgressions should be visited with equal severity on both man and woman.

Resolved, That the objection of indelicacy and impropriety, which is so often brought against woman when she addresses a public audience, comes with a very ill-grace from those who encourage, by their attendance, her appearance on the stage, in the concert, or in feats of the circus.

Resolved, That woman has too long rested satisfied in the circumscribed limits which corrupt customs and a perverted application of the Scriptures have marked out for her, and that it is time she should move in the enlarged sphere which her great Creator has assigned her.

Resolved, That it is the duty of the women of this country to secure to themselves their sacred right to the elective franchise.

Resolved, That the equality of human rights results necessarily from the fact of the identity of the race in capabilities and responsibilities.

Resolved, therefore, That, being invested by the Creator with the same capabilities, and the same consciousness of responsibility for their exercise, it is demonstrably the right and duty of woman, equally with man, to promote every righteous cause by every righteous means; and especially in regard to the great subjects of morals and religion, it is self-evidently her right to participate with her brother in teaching them, both in private and in public, by writing and by speaking, by any instrumentalities proper to be used, and in any assemblies proper to be held; and this being a self-evident truth growing out of the divinely implanted principles of human nature, any custom or authority adverse to it, whether modern or wearing the hoary sanction of antiquity, is to be regarded as a self-evident falsehood, and at war with mankind.

At the last session Lucretia Mott offered and spoke to the following resolution:

Resolved, That the speedy success of our cause depends upon the zealous and untiring efforts of both men and women, for the overthrow of the monopoly of the pulpit, and for the securing to woman an equal participation with men in the various trades, professions, and commerce.

25

Declaration of the Rights of Women

National Woman Suffrage Association, 1876

> *At the centennial of the Declaration of Independence, the National Woman Suffrage Association adopted the following Declaration of the Rights of Women, which protested the treatment of women "in direct opposition to the principles of just government, acknowledged by the United States as its foundations."*

While the Nation is buoyant with patriotism, and all hearts are attuned to praise, it is with sorrow we come to strike the one discordant note, on this hundredth anniversary of our country's birth. When subjects of Kings, Emperors, and Czars, from the Old World, join in our National Jubilee, shall the women of the Republic refuse to lay their hands with benedictions on the nation's head? Surveying America's Exposition, surpassing in magnificence those of London, Paris, and Vienna, shall we not rejoice at the success of the youngest rival among the nations of the earth? May not our hearts, in unison with all, swell with pride at our great achievements as a people; our free speech, free press, free schools, free church, and the rapid progress we have made in material wealth, trade, commerce, and the inventive arts? And we do rejoice, in the success thus far, of our experiment of self-government. Our faith is firm and unwavering in the broad principles of human rights, proclaimed in 1776, not only as abstract truths, but as the corner stones of a republic. Yet, we cannot forget, even in this glad hour, that while all men of every race, and clime, and condition, have been invested with the full rights of citizenship, under our hospitable flag, all women still suffer the degradation of disfranchisement.

The history of our country the past hundred years, has been a series of assumptions and usurpations of power over woman, in direct opposition to the principles of just government, acknowledged by the United States at its foundation, which are:

First. The natural rights of each individual.

Second. The exact equality of these rights.

Third. That these rights, when not delegated by the individual, are retained by the individual.

Fourth. That no person can exercise the rights of others without delegated authority.

Fifth. That the non-use of these rights does not destroy them.

And for the violation of these fundamental principles of our Government, we arraign our rulers on this 4th day of July, 1876,—and these are our Articles of Impeachment.

Bills of Attainder have been passed by the introduction of the word "male" into all the State constitutions, denying to woman the right of suffrage, and thereby making sex a crime—an exercise of power clearly forbidden in Article 1st, Sections 9th and 10th of the United States Constitution.

The Writ of Habeas Corpus, the only protection against lettres de cachet, and all forms of unjust imprisonment, which the Constitution declares "shall not be suspended, except when in cases of rebellion or invasion, the public safety demands it," is held inoperative in every State in the Union, in case of a married woman against her husband,—the marital rights of the husband being in all cases primary, and the rights of the wife secondary.

The Right of Trial by a Jury of One's Peers was so jealously guarded that States refused to ratify the original Constitution, until it was guaranteed by the 6th Amendment. And yet the women of this nation have never been allowed a jury of their peers—being tried in all cases by men native and foreign, educated and ignorant, virtuous and vicious. Young girls have been arraigned in our courts for the crime of infanticide; tried, convicted, hung—victims, perchance, of judge, jurors, advocates—while no woman's voice could be heard in their defence. And not only are women denied a jury of their peers, but in some cases, jury trial altogether. During the war, a woman was tried and hung by military law, in defiance of the 5th Amendment, which specifically declares: "no person shall be held to answer for a capital or otherwise infamous crime, unless on a presentment or indictment of a grand jury, except in cases . . . of persons in actual service in time of war." During the last Presidential campaign, a woman, arrested for voting, was denied the protection of a jury, tried, convicted and sentenced to a fine and costs of prosecution, by the absolute power of a judge of the Supreme Court of the United States.

Taxation Without Representation, the immediate cause of the rebellion of the Colonies against Great Britain, is one of the grievous wrongs the women of this country have suffered during the century. Deploring war, with all the demoralization that follows in its train, we have been taxed to support standing armies, with their waste of life and wealth. Believing in temperance, we have been taxed to support the vice, crime, and pauperism of the Liquor Traffic. While we suffer its wrongs and abuses infinitely more than man, we have no power to protect our sons against this giant evil. During the Temperance Crusade, mothers were arrested, fined, imprisoned, for even praying and singing in the streets, while men blockade the sidewalks with impunity, even on Sunday, with their military parades and political processions. Believing in honesty, we are taxed to support a dangerous army of civilians, buying and selling the offices of government and sacrificing the best interests of the people. And, moreover, we are taxed to support the very legislators, and judges, who make laws, and render decisions adverse to woman. And for refusing to pay such unjust taxation, the houses, lands, bonds, and stock of women, have been seized and sold within the present year, thus proving Lord Coke's assertion, "that the very act of taxing a man's property without his consent, is, in effect, disfranchising him of every civil right."

Unequal Codes for Men and Women. Held by law a perpetual minor, deemed incapable of self-protection, even in the industries of the world, woman is denied equality of rights. The fact of sex, not the quantity or quality of work, in most cases, decides the pay and position; and because of this injustice thousands of fatherless girls are compelled to choose between a life of shame and starvation.

Laws catering to man's vices have created two codes of morals in which penalties are graded according to the political status of the offender. Under such laws, women are fined and imprisoned if found alone in the streets, or in public places of resort, at certain hours. Under the pretence of regulating public morals, police officers seizing the occupants of disreputable houses, march the women in platoons to prison, while the men, partners in their guilt, go free.

While making a show of virtue in forbidding the importation of Chinese women on the Pacific coast for immoral purposes, our rulers, in many states, and even under the shadow of the National Capitol, are now proposing to legalize the sale of American womanhood for the same vile purposes.

Special Legislation for Woman has placed us in a most anomalous position. Women invested with the rights of citizens in one section—voters, jurors, office-holders—crossing an imaginary line, are subjects in the next. In some states, a married woman may hold property and transact business in her own name; in others, her earnings belong to her husband. In some states, a woman may testify against her husband, sue and be sued in the courts; in others, she has no redress in case of damage to person, property, or character. In case of divorce, on account of adultery in the husband, the innocent wife is held to possess no right to children, or property, unless by special decree of the court. But in no state of the Union has the wife the right to her own person, or to any part of the joint earnings of the co-partnership, during the life of her husband. In some States women may enter the law schools and practice in the courts; in others they are forbidden. In some universities, girls enjoy equal educational advantages with boys, while many of the proudest institutions in the land deny them admittance, though the sons of China, Japan and Africa are welcomed there.

But the privileges already granted in the several states are by no means secure. The right of suffrage once exercised by women in certain States and Territories, has been denied by subsequent legislation. A bill is now pending in Congress to disfranchise the women of Utah, thus interfering to deprive United States citizens of the same rights, which the Supreme Court has declared the National Government powerless to protect anywhere. Laws passed after years of untiring effort, guaranteeing married women certain rights of property, and mothers the custody of their children, have been repealed in States where we supposed all was safe. Thus have our most sacred rights been made the football of legislative caprice, proving that a power which grants, as a privilege, what by nature is a right, may withhold the same as a penalty, when deeming it necessary for its own perpetuation.

Representation for Woman has had no place in the nation's thought. Since the incorporation of the thirteen original states, twenty-four have been admitted to the Union, not one of which has recognized woman's right of self-government On this birthday of our national liberties, July 4th, 1876, Colorado, like all her elder sisters, comes into the Union, with the invidious word "male" in her Constitution.

Universal Manhood Suffrage, by establishing an aristocracy of sex, imposes upon the women of this nation a more absolute and cruel despotism than monarchy; in that, woman finds a political master in her father, husband, brother, son. The aristocracies of the old world are based upon birth, wealth, refinement, education, nobility, brave deeds of chivalry; in this nation, on sex alone; exalting brute force above moral power, vice above virtue, ignorance above education, and the son above the mother who bore him.

The Judiciary of the Nation has proved itself but the echo of the party in power, by upholding and enforcing laws that are opposed to the spirit and letter of the Constitution. When the slave power was dominant, the Supreme Court decided that a black man was not a citizen, because he had not the right to vote; and when the Constitution was so amended as to make all persons citizens, the same high tribunal decided that a woman, though a citizen, had not the right to vote. Such vacillating interpretations of constitutional law unsettle our faith in judicial authority, and undermine the liberties of the whole people.

These Articles of Impeachment Against Our Rulers we now submit to the impartial judgment of the people.

To all these wrongs and oppressions woman has not submitted in silence and resignation. From the beginning of the century, when Abigail Adams, the wife of one President and the mother of another, said, "we will not hold ourselves bound to obey laws in which we have no voice or representation," until now, woman's discontent has been steadily increasing, culminating nearly thirty years ago in a simultaneous movement among the women of the nation, demanding the right of suffrage. In making our just demands, a higher motive than the pride of sex inspires us; we feel that national safety and stability depend on the complete recognition of the broad principles of our government. Woman's degraded, helpless position is the weak point in our institutions to-day; a disturbing force everywhere, severing family ties, filling our asylums with the deaf, the dumb, the blind, our prisons with criminals, our cities with drunkenness and prostitution, our homes with disease and death.

It was the boast of the founders of the republic, that the rights for which they contended, were the rights of human nature. If these rights are ignored in the case of one half the people, the nation is surely preparing for its own downfall. Governments try themselves. The recognition of a governing and a governed class is incompatible with the first principles of freedom. Woman has not been a heedless spectator of the events of this century, nor a dull listener to the grand arguments for the equal rights of humanity. From the earliest history of our country, woman has shown equal devotion with man to the cause of freedom, and has stood firmly by his side in its defence. Together, they have made this country what it is. Woman's wealth, thought and labor have cemented the stones of every monument man has reared to liberty.

And now, at the close of a hundred years, as the hour hand of the great clock that marks the centuries points to 1876, we declare our faith in the principles of self-government; our full equality with man in natural rights; that woman was made first for her own happiness, with the absolute right to herself—to all the opportunities and advantages life affords, for her complete development; and we deny that dogma of the centuries, incorporated in the codes of all nations—that woman was made for man—her best interests, in all cases, to be sacrificed to his will.

We ask of our rulers, at this hour, no special favors, no special privileges, no special legislation. We ask justice, we ask equality, we ask that all the civil and political rights that belong to citizens of the United States, be guaranteed to us and our daughters forever.

26

The Inevitability of Women's Suffrage

Carrie Chapmen Catt, 1917

> *Carrie Chapman Catt (1859–1947), President of the National American Woman Suffrage Association, gave the following speech to Congress in 1917. In her address, Catt noted that the principles in the Declaration of Independence had become "the slogans of every movement toward political liberty the world around," and she, too, invoked the principles of the Declaration to push for women's suffrage in the United States.*

Woman suffrage is inevitable. Suffragists knew it before November 4, 1917; opponents afterward. Three distinct causes made it inevitable.

First, the history of our country. Ours is a nation born of revolution, of rebellion against a system of government so securely entrenched in the customs and traditions of human society that in 1776 it seemed impregnable. From the beginning of things, nations had been ruled by kings and for kings, while the people served and paid the cost. The American Revolutionists boldly proclaimed the heresies: "Taxation without representation is tyranny." "Governments derive their just powers from the consent of the governed." The colonists won, and the nation which was established as a result of their victory has held unfailingly that these two fundamental principles of democratic government are not only the spiritual source of our national existence but have been our chief historic pride and at all times the sheet anchor of our liberties.

Eighty years after the Revolution, Abraham Lincoln welded those two maxims into a new one: "Ours is a government of the people, by the people, and for the people." Fifty years more passed and the president of the United States, Woodrow Wilson, in a mighty crisis of the nation, proclaimed to the world: "We are fighting for the things which we have always carried nearest to our hearts: for democracy, for the right of those who submit to authority to have a voice in their own government."

All the way between these immortal aphorisms political leaders have declared unabated faith in their truth. Not one American has arisen to question their logic in the 141 years of our national existence. However stupidly our country may have evaded the logical application at times, it has never swerved from its devotion to the theory of democracy as expressed by those two axioms . . . .

With such a history behind it, how can our nation escape the logic it has never failed to follow, when its last unenfranchised class calls for the vote? Behold our Uncle Sam floating the banner with one hand, "Taxation without representation is tyranny," and with the other seizing the billions of dollars paid in taxes by women to whom he refuses "representation." Behold him again, welcoming the boys of twenty-one and the newly made immigrant citizen to "a voice in their own government" while he denies that fundamental right of democracy to thousands of women public school teachers from whom many of these men learn all they know of citizenship and patriotism, to women college presidents, to women who preach in our pulpits, interpret law in our courts, preside over our hospitals, write books and magazines, and serve in every uplifting moral and social enterprise. Is there a single man who can justify such inequality of treatment, such outrageous discrimination? . . .

Second, the suffrage for women already established in the United States makes women suffrage for the nation inevitable. When Elihu Root, as president of the American Society of International Law, at the eleventh annual meeting in Washington, April 26, 1917, said, "The world cannot be half democratic and half autocratic. It must be all democratic or all Prussian. There can be no compromise," he voiced a general truth. Precisely the same intuition has already taught the blindest and most hostile foe of woman suffrage that our nation cannot long continue a condition under which government in half its territory rests upon the consent of half of the people and in the other half upon the consent of all the people; a condition which grants representation to the taxed in half of its territory and denies it in the other half a condition which permits women in some states to share in the election of the president, senators, and representatives and denies them that privilege in others. It is too obvious to require demonstration that woman suffrage, now covering half our territory, will eventually be ordained in all the nation. No one will deny it. The only question left is when and how will It be completely established.

Third, the leadership of the United States in world democracy compels the enfranchisement of its own women. The maxims of the Declaration were once called "fundamental principles of government." They are now called "American principles" or even "Americanisms." They have become the slogans of every movement toward political liberty the world around, of every effort to widen the suffrage for men or women in any land. Not a people, race, or class striving for freedom is there anywhere in the world that has not made our axioms the chief weapon of the struggle. More, all men and women the world around, with farsighted vision into the verities of things, know that the world tragedy of our day is not now being waged over the assassination of an archduke, nor commercial competition, nor national ambitions, nor the freedom of the seas. It is a death grapple between the forces which deny and those which uphold the truths of the Declaration of Independence.

Do you realize that in no other country in the world with democratic tendencies is suffrage so completely denied as in a considerable number of our own states? There are thirteen black states where no suffrage for women exists, and fourteen others where suffrage for women is more limited than in many foreign countries.

Do you realize that when you ask women to take their cause to state referendum you compel them to do this: that you drive women of education, refinement, achievement, to beg men who cannot read for their political freedom?

Do you realize that such anomalies as a college president asking her janitor to give her a vote are overstraining the patience and driving women to desperation?

Do you realize that women in increasing numbers indignantly resent the long delay in their enfranchisement?

Your party platforms have pledged women suffrage. Then why not be honest, frank friends of our cause, adopt it in reality as your own, make it a party program, and "fight with us"? As a party measure—a measure of all parties—why not put the amendment through Congress and the legislatures? We shall all be better friends, we shall have a happier nation, we women will be free to support loyally the party of our choice, and we shall be far prouder of our history.

"There is one thing mightier than kings and armies"—aye, than Congresses and political parties—"the power of an idea when its time has come to move." The time for woman suffrage has come. The woman's hour has struck. If parties prefer to postpone action longer and thus do battle with this idea, they challenge the inevitable. The idea will not perish; the party which opposes it may. Every delay, every trick, every political dishonesty from now on will antagonize the women of the land more and more, and when the party or parties which have so delayed woman suffrage finally let it come, their sincerity will be doubted and their appeal to the new voters will be met with suspicion. This is the psychology of the situation. Can you afford the risk? Think it over.

We know you will meet opposition. There are a few "women haters" left, a few "old males of the tribe," as Vance Thompson calls them, whose duty they believe it to be to keep women in the places they have carefully picked out for them. Treitschke, made world famous by war literature, said some years ago, "Germany, which knows all about Germany and France, knows far better what is good for Alsace-Lorraine than that miserable people can possibly know." A few American Treitschkes we have who know better than women what is good for them. There are women, too, with "slave souls" and "clinging vines" for backbones. There are female dolls and male dandies. But the world does not wait for such as these, nor does liberty pause to heed the plaint of men and women with a grouch. She does not wait for those who have a special interest to serve, nor a selfish reason for depriving other people of freedom. Holding her torch aloft, liberty is pointing the way onward and upward and saying to America, "Come."

To you and the supporters of our cause in Senate and House, and the number is large, the suffragists of the nation express their grateful thanks. This address is not meant for you. We are more truly appreciative of all you have done than any words can express. We ask you to make a last, hard fight for the amendment during the present session. Since last we asked a vote on this amendment, your position has been fortified by the addition to suffrage territory of Great Britain, Canada, and New York.

Some of you have been too indifferent to give more than casual attention to this question. It is worthy of your immediate consideration. A question big enough to engage the attention of our allies in wartime is too big a question for you to neglect.

Some of you have grown old in party service. Are you willing that those who take your places by and by shall blame you for having failed to keep pace with the world and thus having lost for them a party advantage? Is there any real gain for you, for your party, for your nation by delay? Do you want to drive the progressive men and women out of your party?

Some of you hold to the doctrine of states' rights as applying to woman suffrage. Adherence to that theory will keep the United States far behind all other democratic nations upon this question. A theory which prevents a nation from keeping up with the trend of world progress cannot be justified.

Gentlemen, we hereby petition you, our only designated representatives, to redress our grievances by the immediate passage of the Federal Suffrage Amendment and to use your influence to secure its ratification in your own state, in order that the women of our nation may be endowed with political freedom before the next presidential election, and that our nation may resume its world leadership in democracy.

Woman suffrage is coming—you know it. Will you, Honorable Senators and Members of the House of Representatives, help or hinder it?

27

What is Progress?

Woodrow Wilson, 1913

> Woodrow Wilson (1856–1924) served as president of Princeton University and Governor of New Jersey before winning the U.S. presidential election in 1912. In the following excerpt from his 1913 book The New Freedom, Wilson argued that the political theories undergirding the Declaration and the Constitution were largely irrelevant to the problems of modern government.

... One of the chief benefits I used to derive from being president of a university was that I had the pleasure of entertaining thoughtful men from all over the world. I cannot tell you how much has dropped into my granary by their presence. I had been casting around in my mind for something by which to draw several parts of my political thought together when it was my good fortune to entertain a very interesting Scotsman who had been devoting himself to the philosophical thought of the seventeenth century. His talk was so engaging that it was delightful to hear him speak of anything, and presently there came out of the unexpected region of his thought the thing I had been waiting for. He called my attention to the fact that in every generation all sorts of speculation and thinking tend to fall under the formula of the dominant thought of the age. For example, after the Newtonian Theory of the universe had been developed, almost all thinking tended to express itself in the analogies of the Newtonian Theory, and since the Darwinian Theory has reigned amongst us, everybody is likely to express whatever he wishes to expound in terms of development and accommodation to environment.

Now, it came to me, as this interesting man talked, that the Constitution of the United States had been made under the dominion of the Newtonian Theory. You have only to read the papers of *The Federalist* to see that fact written on every page. They speak of the "checks and balances" of the Constitution, and use to express their idea the simile of the organization of the universe, and particularly of the solar system—how by the attraction of gravitation the various parts are held in their orbits; and then they proceed to represent Congress, the Judiciary, and the President as a sort of imitation of the solar system.

They were only following the English Whigs, who gave Great Britain its modern constitution. Not that those Englishmen analyzed the matter, or had any theory about it; Englishmen care little for theories. It was a Frenchman, Montesquieu, who pointed out to them how faithfully they had copied Newton's description of the mechanism of the heavens.

The makers of our Federal Constitution read Montesquieu with true scientific enthusiasm. They were scientists in their way—the best way of their age—those fathers of the nation. Jefferson wrote of "the laws of Nature, "and then by way of afterthought" and of Nature's God." And they constructed a government as they would have constructed an orrery—to display the laws of nature. Politics in their thought was a variety of mechanics. The Constitution was founded on the law of gravitation. The government was to exist and move by virtue of the efficacy of "checks and balances."

The trouble with the theory is that government is not a machine, but a living thing. It falls, not under the theory of the universe, but under the theory of organic life. It is accountable to Darwin, not to Newton. It is modified by its environment, necessitated by its tasks, shaped to its functions by the sheer pressure of life. No living thing can have its organs offset against each other, as checks, and live. On the contrary, its life is dependent upon their quick co-operation, their ready response to the commands of instinct or intelligence, their amicable community of purpose. Government is not a body of blind forces; it is a body of men, with highly differentiated functions, no doubt, in our modern day, of specialization, with a common task and purpose. Their co-operation is indispensable, their warfare fatal. There can be no successful government without the intimate, instinctive co-ordination of the organs of life and action. This is not theory, but fact, and displays its force as fact, whatever theories may be thrown across its track. Living political constitutions must be Darwinian in structure and in practice. Society is a living organism and must obey the laws of life, not of mechanics; it must develop.

All that progressives ask or desire is permission—in an era when "development," "evolution," is the scientific word—to interpret the Constitution according to the Darwinian principle; all they ask is recognition of the fact that a nation is a living thing and not a machine.

Some citizens of this country have never got beyond the Declaration of Independence, signed in Philadelphia, July 4th, 1776. Their bosoms swell against George III, but they have no consciousness of the war for freedom that is going on to-day.

The Declaration of Independence did not mention the questions of our day. It is of no consequence to us unless we can translate its general terms into examples of the present day and substitute them in some vital way for the examples it itself gives, so concrete, so intimately involved in the circumstances of the day in which it was conceived and written. It is an eminently practical document, meant for the use of practical men; not a thesis for philosophers, but a whip for tyrants; not a theory of government, but a program of action. Unless we can translate it into the questions of our own day, we are not worthy of it, we are not the sons of the sires who acted in response to its challenge.

What form does the contest between tyranny and freedom take to-day? What is the special form of tyranny we now fight? How does it endanger the rights of the people, and what do we mean to do in order to make our contest against it effectual? What are to be the items of our new declaration of independence?

By tyranny, as we now fight it, we mean control of the law, of legislation and adjudication, by organizations which do not represent the people, by means which are private and selfish. We mean, specifically, the conduct of our affairs and the shaping of our legislation in the interest of special bodies of capital and those who organize their use. We mean the alliance, for this purpose, of political machines with selfish business. We mean the exploitation of the people by legal and political means. We have seen many of our governments under these influences cease to be representative governments, cease to be governments representative of the people, and become governments representative of special interests, controlled by machines, which in their turn are not controlled by the people

Sometimes, when I think of the growth of our economic system, it seems to me as if, leaving our law just about where it was before any of the modern inventions or developments took place, we had simply at haphazard extended the family residence, added an office here and a workroom there, and a new set of sleeping rooms there, built up higher on our foundations, and put out little lean-tos on the side, until we have a structure that has no character whatever. Now, the problem is to continue to live in the house and yet change it.

Well, we are architects in our time, and our architects are also engineers. We don't have to stop using a railroad terminal because a new station is being built. We don't have to stop any of the processes of our lives because we are rearranging the structures in which we conduct those processes. What we have to undertake is to systematize the foundations of the house, then to thread all the old parts of the structure with the steel which will be laced together in modern fashion, accommodated to all the modern knowledge of structural strength and elasticity, and then slowly change the partitions, relay the walls, let in the light through new apertures, improve the ventilation; until finally, a generation or two from now, the scaffolding will be taken away, and there will be the family in a great building whose noble architecture will at last be disclosed, where men can live as a single community, co-operative as in a perfected, coordinated beehive, not afraid of any storm of nature, not afraid of any artificial storm, any imitation of thunder and lightning, knowing that the foundations go down to the bedrock of principle, and knowing that whenever they please they can change that plan again and accommodate it as they please to the altering necessities of their lives.

But there are a great many men who don't like the idea. Some wit recently said, in view of the fact that most of our American architects are trained in a certain *Ecole* in Paris, that all American architecture in recent years was either bizarre or "Beaux Arts." I think that our economic architecture is decidedly bizarre; and I am afraid that there is a good deal to learn about matters other than architecture from the same source from which our architects have learned a great many things. I don't mean the School of Fine Arts at Paris, but the experience of France; for from the other side of the water men can now hold up against us the reproach that we have not adjusted our lives to modern conditions to the same extent that they have adjusted theirs. I was very much interested in some of the reasons given by our friends across the Canadian border for being very shy about the reciprocity arrangements. They said: "We are not sure whither these arrangements will lead, and we don't care to associate too closely with the economic conditions of the United States until those conditions are as modern as ours." And when I resented it, and asked for particulars, I had, in regard to many matters, to retire from the debate. Because I found that they had adjusted their regulations of economic development to conditions we had not yet found a way to meet in the United States.

Well, we have started now at all events. The procession is under way. The stand-patter doesn't know there is a procession. He is asleep in the back part of his house. He doesn't know that the road is resounding with the tramp of men going to the front. And when he wakes up, the country will be empty. He will be deserted, and he will wonder what has happened. Nothing has happened. The world has been going on. The world has a habit of going on. The world has a habit of leaving those behind who won't go with it. The world has always neglected stand-patters. And, therefore, the stand-patter does not excite my indignation; he excites my sympathy. He is going to be so lonely before it is all over. And we are good fellows, we are good company; why doesn't he come along? We are not going to do him any harm. We are going to show him a good time. We are going to climb the slow road until it reaches some upland where the air is fresher, where the whole talk of mere politicians is stilled, where men can look in each other's faces and see that there is nothing to conceal, that all they have to talk about they are willing to talk about in the open and talk about with each other; and whence, looking back over the road, we shall see at last that we have fulfilled our promise to mankind. We had said to all the world, "America was created to break every kind of monopoly, and to set men free, upon a footing of equality, upon a footing of opportunity, to match their brains and their energies." And now we have proved that we meant it.

28

Speech on the Fourth of July

Calvin Coolidge, 1926

> *Calvin Coolidge (1872–1933) gave the following address on the one hundred fiftieth anniversary of the Declaration of Independence. Coolidge, who served as president from 1923 to 1929, used the occasion to consider the meaning and place of the Declaration in the modern world. In some respects, Coolidge insisted, there was an "exceeding finality" to the ideas in the Declaration beyond which a nation could not progress.*

We meet to celebrate the birthday of America. The coming of a new life always excites our interest. Although we know in the case of the individual that it has been an infinite repetition reaching back beyond our vision, that only makes it the more wonderful. But how our interest and wonder increase when we behold the miracle of the birth of a new nation. It is to pay our tribute of reverence and respect to those who participated in such a mighty event that we annually observe the fourth day of July. Whatever may have been the impression created by the news which went out from this city on that summer day in 1776, there can be no doubt as to the estimate which is now placed upon it. At the end of 150 years the four corners of the earth unite in coming to Philadelphia as to a holy shrine in grateful acknowledgement of a service so great, which a few inspired men here rendered to humanity, that it is still the preeminent support of free government throughout the world.

Although a century and a half measured in comparison with the length of human experience is but a short time, yet measured in the life of governments and nations it ranks as a very respectable period. Certainly enough time has elapsed to demonstrate with a great deal of thoroughness the value of our institutions and their dependability as rules for the regulation of human conduct and the advancement of civilization. They have been in existence long enough to become very well seasoned. They have met, and met successfully, the test of experience.

It is not so much then for the purpose of undertaking to proclaim new theories and principles that this annual celebration is maintained, but rather to reaffirm and reestablish those old theories and principles which time and the unerring logic of events have demonstrated to be sound. Amid all the clash of conflicting interests, amid all the welter of partisan politics, every American can turn for solace and consolation to the Declaration of independence and the Constitution of the United States with the assurance and confidence that those two great charters of freedom and justice remain firm and unshaken. Whatever perils appear, whatever dangers threaten, the Nation remains secure in the knowledge that the ultimate application of the law of the land will provide an adequate defense and protection.

It is little wonder that people at home and abroad consider Independence Hall as hallowed ground and revere the Liberty Bell as a sacred relic. That pile of bricks and mortar, that mass of metal, might appear to the uninstructed as only the outgrown meeting place and the shattered bell of a former time, useless now because of more modern conveniences, but to those who know they have become consecrated by the use which men have made of them. They have long been identified with a great cause. They are the framework of a spiritual event. The world looks upon them, because of their associations of one hundred and fifty years ago, as it looks upon the Holy Land because of what took place there nineteen hundred years ago. Through use for a righteous purpose they have become sanctified.

It is not here necessary to examine in detail the causes which led to the American Revolution. In their immediate occasion they were largely economic. The colonists objected to the navigation laws which interfered with their trade, they denied the power of Parliament to impose taxes which they were obliged to pay, and they therefore resisted the royal governors and the royal forces which were sent to secure obedience to these laws. But the conviction is inescapable that a new civilization had come, a new spirit had arisen on this side of the Atlantic more advanced and more developed in its regard for the rights of the individual than that which characterized the Old World. Life in a new and open country had aspirations which could not be realized in any subordinate position. A separate establishment was ultimately inevitable. It had been decreed by the very laws of human nature. Man everywhere has an unconquerable desire to be the master of his own destiny.

We are obliged to conclude that the Declaration of Independence represented the movement of a people. It was not, of course, a movement from the top. Revolutions do not come from that direction. It was not without the support of many of the most respectable people in the Colonies, who were entitled to all the consideration that is given to breeding, education, and possessions. It had the support of another element of great significance and importance to which I shall later refer. But the preponderance of all those who occupied a position which took on the aspect of aristocracy did not approve of the Revolution and held toward it an attitude either of neutrality or open hostility. It was in no sense a rising of the oppressed and downtrodden. It brought no scum to the surface, for the reason that colonial society had developed no scum. The great body of the people were accustomed to privations, but they were free from depravity. If they had poverty, it was not of the hopeless kind that afflicts great cities, but the inspiring kind that marks the spirit of the pioneer. The American Revolution represented the informed and mature convictions of a great mass of independent, liberty-loving, God-fearing people who knew their rights, and possessed the courage to dare to maintain them.

The Continental Congress was not only composed of great men, but it represented a great people. While its members did not fail to exercise a remarkable leadership, they were equally observant of their representative capacity. They were industrious in encouraging their constituents to instruct them to support independence. But until such instructions were given they were inclined to withhold action.

While North Carolina has the honor of first authorizing its delegates to concur with other Colonies in declaring independence, it was quickly followed by South Carolina and Georgia, which also gave general instructions broad enough to include such action. But the first instructions which unconditionally directed its delegates to declare for independence came from the great Commonwealth of Virginia. These were immediately followed by Rhode Island and Massachusetts, while the other Colonies, with the exception of New York, soon adopted a like course.

This obedience of the delegates to the wishes of their constituents, which in some cases caused them to modify their previous positions, is a matter of great significance. It reveals an orderly process of government in the first place; but more than that, it demonstrates that the Declaration of Independence was the result of the seasoned and deliberate thought of the dominant portion of the people of the Colonies. Adopted after long discussion and as the result of the duly authorized expression of the preponderance of public opinion, it did not partake of dark intrigue or hidden conspiracy. It was well advised. It had about it nothing of the lawless and disordered nature of a riotous insurrection. It was maintained on a plane which rises above the ordinary conception of rebellion. It was in no sense a radical movement but took on the dignity of a resistance to illegal usurpations. It was conservative and represented the action of the colonists to maintain their constitutional rights which from time immemorial had been guaranteed to them under the law of the land.

When we come to examine the action of the Continental Congress in adopting the Declaration of Independence in the light of what was set out in that great document and in the light of succeeding events, we can not escape the conclusion that it had a much broader and deeper significance than a mere secession of territory and the establishment of a new nation. Events of that nature have been taking place since the dawn of history. One empire after another has arisen, only to crumble away as its constituent parts separated from each other and set up independent governments of their own. Such actions long ago became commonplace. They have occurred too often to hold the attention of the world and command the admiration and reverence of humanity. There is something beyond the establishment of a new nation, great as that event would be, in the Declaration of Independence which has ever since caused it to be regarded as one of the great charters that not only was to liberate America but was everywhere to ennoble humanity.

It was not because it was proposed to establish a new nation, but because it was proposed to establish a nation on new principles, that July 4, 1776, has come to be regarded as one of the greatest days in history. Great ideas do not burst upon the world unannounced. They are reached by a gradual development over a length of time usually proportionate to their importance. This is especially true of the principles laid down in the Declaration of Independence. Three very definite propositions were set out in its preamble regarding the nature of mankind and therefore of government. These were the doctrine that all men are created equal, that they are endowed with certain inalienable rights, and that therefore the source of the just powers of government must be derived from the consent of the governed

If no one is to be accounted as born into a superior station, if there is to be no ruling class, and if all possess rights which can neither be bartered away nor taken from them by any earthly power, it follows as a matter of course that the practical authority of the Government has to rest on the consent of the governed. While these principles were not altogether new in political action, and were very far from new in political speculation, they had never been assembled before and declared in such a combination. But remarkable as this may be, it is not the chief distinction of the Declaration of Independence. The importance of political speculation is not to be under-estimated, as I shall presently disclose. Until the idea is developed and the plan made there can be no action.

It was the fact that our Declaration of Independence containing these immortal truths was the political action of a duly authorized and constituted representative public body in its sovereign capacity, supported by the force of general opinion and by the armies of Washington already in the field, which makes it the most important civil document in the world. It was not only the principles declared, but the fact that therewith a new nation was born which was to be founded upon those principles and which from that time forth in its development has actually maintained those principles, that makes this pronouncement an incomparable event in the history of government. It was an assertion that a people had arisen determined to make every necessary sacrifice for the support of these truths and by their practical application bring the War of Independence to a successful conclusion and adopt the Constitution of the United States with all that it has meant to civilization.

The idea that the people have a right to choose their own rulers was not new in political history. It was the foundation of every popular attempt to depose an undesirable king. This right was set out with a good deal of detail by the Dutch when as early as July 26, 1581, they declared their independence of Philip of Spain. In their long struggle with the Stuarts the British people asserted the same principles, which finally culminated in the Bill of Rights deposing the last of that house and placing William and Mary on the throne. In each of these cases sovereignty through divine right was displaced by sovereignty through the consent of the people. Running through the same documents, though expressed in different terms, is the clear inference of inalienable rights. But we should search these charters in vain for an assertion of the doctrine of equality. This principle had not before appeared as an official political declaration of any nation. It was profoundly revolutionary. It is one of the corner stones of American institutions.

But if these truths to which the declaration refers have not before been adopted in their combined entirety by national authority, it is a fact that they had been long pondered and often expressed in political speculation. It is generally assumed that French thought had some effect upon our public mind during Revolutionary days. This may have been true. But the principles of our declaration had been under discussion in the Colonies for nearly two generations before the advent of the French political philosophy that characterized the middle of the eighteenth century. In fact, they come from an earlier date. A very positive echo of what the Dutch had done in 1581, and what the English were preparing to do, appears in the assertion of the Rev. Thomas Hooker of Connecticut as early as 1638, when he said in a sermon before the General Court that—

"The foundation of authority is laid in the free consent of the people"

"The choice of public magistrates belongs unto the people by God's own allowance."

This doctrine found wide acceptance among the nonconformist clergy who later made up the Congregational Church. The great apostle of this movement was the Rev. John Wise, of Massachusetts. He was one of the leaders of the revolt against the royal governor Andros in 1687, for which he suffered imprisonment. He was a liberal in ecclesiastical controversies. He appears to have been familiar with the writings of the political scientist, Samuel Pufendorf, who was born in Saxony in 1632. Wise published a treatise, entitled "The Church's Quarrel Espoused," in 1710, which was amplified in another publication in 1717. In it he dealt with the principles of civil government. His works were reprinted in 1772 and have been declared to have been nothing less than a textbook of liberty for our Revolutionary fathers.

While the written word was the foundation, it is apparent that the spoken word was the vehicle for convincing the people. This came with great force and wide range from the successors of Hooker and Wise, It was carried on with a missionary spirit which did not fail to reach the Scotch-Irish of North Carolina, showing its influence by significantly making that Colony the first to give instructions to its delegates looking to independence. This preaching reached the neighborhood of Thomas Jefferson, who acknowledged that his "best ideas of democracy" had been secured at church meetings.

That these ideas were prevalent in Virginia is further revealed by the Declaration of Rights, which was prepared by George Mason and presented to the general assembly on May 27, 1776. This document asserted popular sovereignty and inherent natural rights, but confined the doctrine of equality to the assertion that "All men are created equally free and independent." It can scarcely be imagined that Jefferson was unacquainted with what had been done in his own Commonwealth of Virginia when he took up the task of drafting the Declaration of Independence. But these thoughts can very largely be traced back to what John Wise was writing in 1710. He said, "Every man must be acknowledged equal to every man." Again, "The end of all good government is to cultivate humanity and promote the happiness of all and the good of every man in all his rights, his life, liberty, estate, honor, and so forth. . . ." And again, "For as they have a power every man in his natural state, so upon combination they can and do bequeath this power to others and settle it according as their united discretion shall determine." And still again, "Democracy is Christ's government in church and state." Here was the doctrine of equality, popular sovereignty, and the substance of the theory of inalienable rights clearly asserted by Wise at the opening of the eighteenth century, just as we have the principle of the consent of the governed stated by Hooker as early as 1638.

When we take all these circumstances into consideration, it is but natural that the first paragraph of the Declaration of Independence should open with a reference to Nature's God and should close in the final paragraphs with an appeal to the Supreme Judge of the world and an assertion of a firm reliance on Divine Providence. Coming from these sources, having as it did this background, it is no wonder that Samuel Adams could say "The people seem to recognize this resolution as though it were a decree promulgated from heaven."

No one can examine this record and escape the conclusion that in the great outline of its principles the Declaration was the result of the religious teachings of the preceding period. The profound philosophy which Jonathan Edwards applied to theology, the popular preaching of George Whitefield, had aroused the thought and stirred the people of the Colonies in preparation for this great event. No doubt the speculations which had been going on in England, and especially on the Continent, lent their influence to the general sentiment of the times. Of course, the world is always influenced by all the experience and all the thought of the past. But when we come to a contemplation of the immediate conception of the principles of human relationship which went into the Declaration of Independence we are not required to extend our search beyond our own shores. They are found in the texts, the sermons, and the writings of the early colonial clergy who were earnestly undertaking to instruct their congregations in the great mystery of how to live. They preached equality because they believed in the fatherhood of God and the brotherhood of man. They justified freedom by the text that we are all created in the divine image, all partakers of the divine spirit.

Placing every man on a plane where he acknowledged no superiors, where no one possessed any right to rule over him, he must inevitably choose his own rulers through a system of self-government. This was their theory of democracy. In those days such doctrines would scarcely have been permitted to flourish and spread in any other country. This was the purpose which the fathers cherished. In order that they might have freedom to express these thoughts and opportunity to put them into action, whole congregations with their pastors had migrated to the colonies. These great truths were in the air that our people breathed. Whatever else we may say of it, the Declaration of Independence was profoundly American.

If this apprehension of the facts be correct, and the documentary evidence would appear to verify it, then certain conclusions are bound to follow. A spring will cease to flow if its source be dried up; a tree will wither if its roots be destroyed. In its main features the Declaration of Independence is a great spiritual document. It is a declaration not of material but of spiritual conceptions. Equality, liberty, popular sovereignty, the rights of man these are not elements which we can see and touch. They are ideals. They have their source and their roots in the religious convictions. They belong to the unseen world. Unless the faith of the American people in these religious convictions is to endure, the principles of our Declaration will perish. We can not continue to enjoy the result if we neglect and abandon the cause.

We are too prone to overlook another conclusion. Governments do not make ideals, but ideals make governments. This is both historically and logically true. Of course the government can help to sustain ideals and can create institutions through which they can be the better observed, but their source by their very nature is in the people. The people have to bear their own responsibilities. There is no method by which that burden can be shifted to the government. It is not the enactment, but the observance of laws, that creates the character of a nation.

About the Declaration there is a finality that is exceedingly restful. It is often asserted that the world has made a great deal of progress since 1776, that we have had new thoughts and new experiences which have given us a great advance over the people of that day, and that we may therefore very well discard their conclusions for something more modern. But that reasoning can not be applied to this great charter. If all men are created equal, that is final. If they are endowed with inalienable rights, that is final. If governments derive their just powers from the consent of the governed, that is final. No advance, no progress can be made beyond these propositions. If anyone wishes to deny their truth or their soundness, the only direction in which he can proceed historically is not forward, but backward toward the time when there was no equality, no rights of the individual, no rule of the people. Those who wish to proceed in that direction can not lay claim to progress. They are reactionary. Their ideas are not more modern, but more ancient, than those of the Revolutionary fathers.

In the development of its institutions America can fairly claim that it has remained true to the principles which were declared 150 years ago. In all the essentials we have achieved an equality which was never possessed by any other people. Even in the less important matter of material possessions we have secured a wider and wider distribution of wealth. The rights of the individual are held sacred and protected by constitutional guaranties, which even the Government itself is bound not to violate. If there is any one thing among us that is established beyond question, it is self-government--the right of the people to rule. If there is any failure in respect to any of these principles, it is because there is a failure on the part of individuals to observe them. We hold that the duly authorized expression of the will of the people has a divine sanction. But even in that we come back to the theory of John Wise that "Democracy is Christ's government." The ultimate sanction of law rests on the righteous authority of the Almighty.

On an occasion like this a great temptation exists to present evidence of the practical success of our form of democratic republic at home and the ever-broadening acceptance it is securing abroad. Although these things are well known, their frequent consideration is an encouragement and an inspiration. But it is not results and effects so much as sources and causes that I believe it is even more necessary constantly to contemplate. Ours is a government of the people It represents their will. Its officers may sometimes go astray, but that is not a reason for criticizing the principles of our institutions. The real heart of the American Government depends upon the heart of the people. It is from that source that we must look for all genuine reform. It is to that cause that we must ascribe all our results.

It was in the contemplation of these truths that the fathers made their declaration and adopted their Constitution. It was to establish a free government, which must not be permitted to degenerate into the unrestrained authority of a mere majority or the unbridled weight of a mere influential few. They undertook to balance these interests against each other and provide the three separate independent branches, the executive, the legislative, and the judicial departments of the Government, with checks against each other in order that neither one might encroach upon the other. These are our guaranties of liberty. As a result of these methods enterprise has been duly protected from confiscation, the people have been free from oppression, and there has been an ever-broadening and deepening of the humanities of life.

Under a system of popular government there will always be those who will seek for political preferment by clamoring for reform. While there is very little of this which is not sincere, there is a large portion that is not well informed. In my opinion very little of just criticism can attach to the theories and principles of our institutions. There is far more danger of harm than there is hope of good in any radical changes. We do need a better understanding and comprehension of them and a better knowledge of the foundations of government in general. Our forefathers came to certain conclusions and decided upon certain courses of action which have been a great blessing to the world. Before we can understand their conclusions we must go back and review the course which they followed. We must think the thoughts which they thought. Their intellectual life centered around the meeting-house. They were intent upon religious worship. While there were always among them men of deep learning, and later those who had comparatively large possessions, the mind of the people was not so much engrossed in how much they knew, or how much they had, as in how they were going to live. While scantily provided with other literature, there was a wide acquaintance with the Scriptures. Over a period as great as that which measures the existence of our independence they were subject to this discipline not only in their religious life and educational training, but also in their political thought. They were a people who came under the influence of a great spiritual development and acquired a great moral power.

No other theory is adequate to explain or comprehend the Declaration of Independence. It is the product of the spiritual insight of the people. We live in an age of science and of abounding accumulation of material things. These did not create our Declaration. Our Declaration created them. The things of the spirit come first. Unless we cling to that, all our material prosperity, overwhelming though it may appear, will turn to a barren sceptre in our grasp. If we are to maintain the great heritage which has been bequeathed to us, we must be like-minded as the fathers who created it. We must not sink into a pagan materialism. We must cultivate the reverence which they had for the things that are holy. We must follow the spiritual and moral leadership which they showed. We must keep replenished, that they may glow with a more compelling flame, the altar fires before which they worshiped.

29

Commonwealth Club Address

Franklin Roosevelt, 1932

> *During the 1932 presidential campaign, Franklin Roosevelt (1882–1945) delivered the following address at the Commonwealth Club in San Francisco, California. In his remarks, which primarily concerned economic policy during the Great Depression, Roosevelt appealed to the Declaration of Independence and insisted that in America the "task of statesmanship has always been the redefinition of these rights [to life, liberty, and the pursuit of happiness] in terms of a changing and growing social order."*

I count it a privilege to be invited to address the Commonwealth Club. It has stood in the life of this city and State, and it is perhaps accurate to add, the nation, as a group of citizen leaders interested in fundamental problems of government, and chiefly concerned with achievement of progress in government through non-partisan means. The privilege of addressing you, therefore, in the heat of a political campaign, is great. I want to respond to your courtesy in terms consistent with your policy.

I want to speak not of politics but of government. I want to speak not of parties, but of universal principles. They are not political, except in that larger sense in which a great American once expressed a definition of politics, that nothing in all of human life is foreign to the science of politics.

I do want to give you, however, a recollection of a long life spent for a large part in public office. Some of my conclusions and observations have been deeply accentuated in these past few weeks. I have traveled far—from Albany to the Golden Gate. I have seen many people, and heard many things, and today, when in a sense my journey has reached the half-way mark, I am glad of the opportunity to discuss with you what it all means to me.

Sometimes, my friends, particularly in years such as these, the hand of discouragement falls upon us. It seems that things are in a rut, fixed, settled, that the world has grown old and tired and very much out of joint. This is the mood of depression, of dire and weary depression.

But then we look around us in America, and everything tells us that we are wrong. America is new. It is the process of change and development. It has the great potentialities of youth and particularly is this true of the great West, and of this coast, and of California.

I would not have you feel that I regard this as in any sense a new community. I have traveled in many parts of the world, but never have I felt the arresting thought of the change and development more than here, where the old, mystic East would seem to be near to us, where the currents of life and thought and commerce of the whole world meet us. This factor alone is sufficient to cause man to stop and think of the deeper meaning of things, when he stands in this community.

But more than that, I appreciate that the membership of this club consists of men who are thinking in terms beyond the immediate present, beyond their own immediate tasks, beyond their own individual interests. I want to invite you, therefore, to consider with me in the large, some of the relationships of government and economic life that go deeply into our daily lives, our happiness, our future and our security.

The issue of government has always been whether individual men and women will have to serve some system of government or economics, or whether a system of government and economics exists to serve individual men and women. This question has persistently dominated the discussion of government for many generations. On questions relating to these things men have differed, and for time immemorial it is probable that honest men will continue to differ.

The final word belongs to no man; yet we can still believe in change and in progress. Democracy, as a dear old friend of mine in Indiana, Meredith Nicholson, has called it, is a quest, a never ending seeking for better things, and in the seeking for these things and the striving for them, there are many roads to follow. But, if we map the course of these roads, we find that there are only two general directions.

When we look about us, we are likely to forget how hard people have worked to win the privilege of government. The growth of the national governments of Europe was a struggle for the development of a centralized force in the nation, strong enough to impose peace upon ruling barons. In many instances the victory of the central government, the creation of a strong central government, was a haven of refuge to the individual. The people preferred the master far away to the exploitation and cruelty of the smaller master near at hand.

But the creators of national government were perforce—ruthless men. They were often cruel in their methods, but they did strive steadily toward something that society needed and very much wanted, a strong central State able to keep the peace, to stamp out civil war, to put the unruly nobleman in his place, and to permit the bulk of individuals to live safely. The man of ruthless force had his place in developing a pioneer country, just as he did in fixing the power of the central government in the development of the nations. Society paid him well for his services and its development. When the development among the nations of Europe, however, had been completed, ambition and ruthlessness, having served their term, tended to overstep their mark.

There came a growing feeling that government was conducted for the benefit of a few who thrived unduly at the expense of all. The people sought a balancing—a limiting force. There came gradually, through town councils, trade guilds, national parliaments by constitution and by popular participation and control, limitations on arbitrary power.

Another factor that tended to limit the power of those who ruled, was the rise of the ethical conception that a ruler bore a responsibility for the welfare of his subjects.

The American colonies were born in this struggle. The American Revolution was a turning point in it. After the Revolution the struggle continued and shaped itself in the public life of the country. There were those who because they had seen the confusion which attended the years of war for American independence surrendered to the belief that popular government was essentially dangerous and essentially unworkable. They were honest people, my friends, and we cannot deny that their experience had warranted some measure of fear. The most brilliant, honest and able exponent of this point of view was Hamilton. He was too impatient of slow-moving methods. Fundamentally he believed that the safety of the republic lay in the autocratic strength of its government, that the destiny of individuals was to serve that government, and that fundamentally a great and strong group of central institutions, guided by a small group of able and public spirited citizens, could best direct all government.

But Mr. Jefferson, in the summer of 1776, after drafting the Declaration of Independence turned his mind to the same problem and took a different view. He did not deceive himself with outward forms. Government to him was a means to an end, not an end in itself; it might be either a refuge and a help or a threat and a danger, depending on the circumstances. We find him carefully analyzing the society for which he was to organize a government. "We have no paupers. The great mass of our population is of laborers, our rich who cannot live without labor, either manual or professional, being few and of moderate wealth. Most of the laboring class possess property, cultivate their own lands, have families and from the demand for their labor, are enabled to exact from the rich and the competent such prices as enable them to feed abundantly, clothe above mere decency, to labor moderately and raise their families."

These people, he considered, had two sets of rights, those of "personal competency" and those involved in acquiring and possessing property. By "personal competency" he meant the right of free thinking, freedom of forming and expressing opinions, and freedom of personal living, each man according to his own rights. To insure the first set of rights, a government must so order its functions as not to interfere with the individual. But even Jefferson realized that the exercise of property rights might so interfere with the rights of the individual that the government, without whose assistance the property rights could not exist, must intervene, not to destroy individualism, but to protect it.

You are familiar with the great political duel which followed; and how Hamilton, and his friends, building toward a dominant centralized power were at length defeated in the great election of 1800, by Mr. Jefferson's party. Out of that duel came the two parties, Republican and Democratic, as we know them today.

So began, in American political life, the new day, the day of the individual against the system, the day in which individualism was made the great watchword of American life. The happiest of economic conditions made that day long and splendid. On the Western frontier, land was substantially free. No one, who did not shirk the task of earning a living, was entirely without opportunity to do so. Depressions could, and did, come and go; but they could not alter the fundamental fact that most of the people lived partly by selling their labor and partly by extracting their livelihood from the soil, so that starvation and dislocation were practically impossible. At the very worst there was always the possibility of climbing into a covered wagon and moving west where the untilled prairies afforded a haven for men to whom the East did not provide a place. So great were our natural resources that we could offer this relief not only to our own people, but to the distressed of all the world; we could invite immigration from Europe, and welcome it with open arms. Traditionally, when a depression came a new section of land was opened in the West; and even our temporary misfortune served our manifest destiny.

It was in the middle of the nineteenth century that a new force was released and a new dream created. The force was what is called the industrial revolution, the advance of steam and machinery and the rise of the forerunners of the modern industrial plant. The dream was the dream of an economic machine, able to raise the standard of living for everyone; to bring luxury within the reach of the humblest; to annihilate distance by steam power and later by electricity, and to release everyone from the drudgery of the heaviest manual toil. It was to be expected that this would necessarily affect government. Heretofore, government had merely been called upon to produce conditions within which people could live happily, labor peacefully, and rest secure. Now it was called upon to aid in the consummation of this new dream. There was, however, a shadow over the dream. To be made real, it required use of the talents of men of tremendous will and tremendous ambition, since by no other force could the problems of financing and engineering and new developments be brought to a consummation.

So manifest were the advantages of the machine age, however, that the United States fearlessly, cheerfully, and, I think, rightly, accepted the bitter with the sweet. It was thought that no price was too high to pay for the advantages which we could draw from a finished industrial system. This history of the last half century is accordingly in large measure a history of a group of financial Titans, whose methods were not scrutinized with too much care, and who were honored in proportion as they produced the results, irrespective of the means they used. The financiers who pushed the railroads to the Pacific were always ruthless, often wasteful, and frequently corrupt; but they did build railroads, and we have them today. It has been estimated that the American investor paid the American railway system more than three times over in the process; but despite this fact the net advantage was to the United States. As long as we had free land; as long as population was growing by leaps and bounds; as long as our industrial plants were insufficient to supply our own needs, society chose to give the ambitious man free play and unlimited reward provided only that he produced the economic plant so much desired. During this period of expansion, there was equal opportunity for all and the business of government was not to interfere but to assist in the development of industry. This was done at the request of businessmen themselves. The tariff was originally imposed for the purpose of "fostering our infant industry," a phrase I think the older among you will remember as a political issue not so long ago. The railroads were subsidized, sometimes by grants of money, oftener by grants of land; some of the most valuable oil lands in the United States were granted to assist the financing of the railroad which pushed through the Southwest. A nascent merchant marine was assisted by grants of money, or by mail subsidies, so that our stream shipping might ply the seven seas. Some of my friends tell me that they do not want the government in business. With this I agree; but I wonder whether they realize the implications of the past. For while it has been American doctrine that the government must not go into business in competition with private enterprises, still it has been traditional particularly in Republican Administrations for business urgently to ask the government to put at private disposal all kinds of government assistance. The same man who tells you that he does not want to see the government interfere in business—and he means it, and has plenty of good reasons for saying so—is the first to go to Washington and ask the government for a prohibitory tariff on his product. When things get just bad enough—as they did two years ago—he will go with equal speed to the United States government and ask for a loan; and the Reconstruction Finance Corporation is the outcome of it. Each group has sought protection from the government for its own special interests, without realizing that the function of government must be to favor no small group at the expense of its duty to protect the rights of personal freedom and of private property of all its citizens.

A glance at the situation today only too clearly indicates that equality of opportunity as we have known it no longer exists. Our industrial plant is built; the problem just now is whether under existing conditions it is not overbuilt. Our last frontier has long since been reached, and there is practically no more free land. More than half of our people do not live on the farms or on lands and cannot derive a living by cultivating their own property. There is no safety valve in the form of a Western prairie to which those thrown out of work by the Eastern economic machines can go for a new start. We are not able to invite the immigration from Europe to share our endless plenty. We are now providing a drab living for our own people.

Our system of constantly rising tariffs has at last reacted against us to the point of closing our Canadian frontier on the north, our European markets on the east, many of our Latin American markets to the south, and a goodly proportion of our Pacific markets on the west, through the retaliatory tariffs of those countries. It has forced many of our great industrial institutions who exported their surplus production to such countries, to establish plants in such countries, within the tariff walls. This has resulted in the reduction of the operation of their American plants, and opportunity for employment.

Just as freedom to farm has ceased, so also the opportunity in business has narrowed. It still is true that men can start small enterprises, trusting to native shrewdness and ability to keep abreast of competitors; but area after area has been pre-empted altogether by the great corporations, and even in the fields which still have no great concerns, the small man starts under a handicap. The unfeeling statistics of the past three decades show that the independent businessman is running a losing race. Perhaps he is forced to the wall; perhaps he cannot command credit; perhaps he is "squeezed out," in Mr. Wilson's words, by highly organized corporate competitors, as your corner grocery man can tell you. Recently a careful study was made of the concentration of business in the United States. It showed that our economic life was dominated by some six hundred odd corporations who controlled two-thirds of American industry. Ten million small businessmen divided the other third. More striking still, it appeared that if the process of concentration goes on at the same rate, at the end of another century we shall have all American industry controlled by a dozen corporations, and run by perhaps a hundred men. But plainly, we are steering a steady course toward economic oligarchy, if we are not there already.

Clearly, all this calls for a re-appraisal of values. A mere builder of more industrial plants, a creator of more railroad systems, an organizer of more corporations, is as likely to be a danger as a help. The day of the great promoter or the financial Titan, to whom we granted everything if only he would build, or develop, is over. Our task now is not discovery, or exploitation of natural resources, or necessarily producing more goods. It is the soberer, less dramatic business of administering resources and plants already in hand, of seeking to reestablish foreign markets for our surplus production, of meeting the problem of under consumption, of adjusting production to consumption, of distributing wealth and products more equitably, of adapting existing economic organizations to the service of the people. The day of enlightened administration has come.

Just as in older times the central government was first a haven of refuge, and then a threat, so now in a closer economic system the central and ambitious financial unit is no longer a servant of national desire, but a danger. I would draw the parallel one step farther. We did not think because national government had become a threat in the 18th century that therefore we should abandon the principle of national government. Nor today should we abandon the principle of strong economic units called corporations, merely because their power is susceptible of easy abuse. In other times we dealt with the problem of an unduly ambitious central government. So today we are modifying and controlling our economic units.

As I see it, the task of government in its relation to business is to assist the development of an economic declaration of rights, an economic constitutional order. This is the common task of statesman and businessman. It is the minimum requirement of a more permanently safe order of things.

Every man has a right to life; and this means that he has also a right to make a comfortable living. He may by sloth or crime decline to exercise that right; but it may not be denied him. We have no actual famine or dearth; our industrial and agricultural mechanism can produce enough and to spare. Our government formal and informal, political and economic, owes to every one an avenue to possess himself of a portion of that plenty sufficient for his needs, through his own work.

Every man has a right to his own property, which means a right to be assured, to the fullest extent attainable, in the safety of his savings. By no other means can men carry the burdens of those parts of life which, in the nature of things, afford no chance of labor; childhood, sickness, old age. In all thought of property, this right is paramount; all other property rights must yield to it. If, in accord with this principle, we must restrict the operations of the speculator, the manipulator, even the financier, I believe we must accept the restriction as needful, not to hamper individualism but to protect it.

These two requirements must be satisfied, in the main, by the individuals who claim and hold control of the great industrial and financial combinations, which dominate so large a part of our industrial life. They have undertaken to be not businessmen, but princes—princes of property. I am not prepared to say that the system which produces them is wrong. I am very clear that they must fearlessly and competently assume the responsibility which goes with the power. So many enlightened businessmen know this that the statement would be little more than a platitude, were it not for an added implication.

This implication is, briefly, that the responsible heads of finance and industry instead of acting each for himself, must work together to achieve the common end. They must, where necessary, sacrifice this or that private advantage; and in reciprocal self-denial must seek a general advantage. It is here that formal government—political government, if you choose, comes in. Whenever in the pursuit of this objective the lone wolf, the unethical competitor, the reckless promoter, the Ishmael or Insull whose hand is against every man's, declines to join in achieving an end recognized as being for the public welfare, and threatens to drag the industry back to a state of anarchy, the government may properly be asked to apply restraint. Likewise, should the group ever use its collective power contrary to the public welfare, the government must be swift to enter and protect the public interest.

The government should assume the function of economic regulation only as a last resort, to be tried only when private initiative, inspired by high responsibility, with such assistance and balance as government can give, has finally failed. As yet there has been no final failure, because there has been no attempt; and I decline to assume that this nation is unable to meet the situation.

The final term of the high contract was for liberty and the pursuit of happiness. We have learnt a great deal of both in the past century. We know that individual liberty and individual happiness mean nothing unless both are ordered in the sense that one man's meat is not another man's poison. We know that the old "rights of personal competency—the right to read, to think, to speak, to choose and live a mode of life, must be respected at all hazards. We know that liberty to do anything which deprives others of those elemental rights is outside the protection of any compact; and that government in this regard is the maintenance of a balance, within which every individual may have a place if he will take it; in which every individual may find safety if he wishes it; in which every individual may attain such power as his ability permits, consistent with his assuming the accompanying responsibility.

Faith in America, faith in our tradition of personal responsibilities, faith in our institutions, faith in ourselves demands that we recognize the new terms of the old social contract. We shall fulfill them, as we fulfilled the obligation of the apparent Utopia which Jefferson imagined for us in 1776, and which Jefferson, Roosevelt and Wilson sought to bring to realization. We must do so, lest a rising tide of misery engendered by our common failure, engulf us all. But failure is not an American habit; and in the strength of great hope we must all shoulder our common load.

30

Speech at the Bicentennial of the Constitution

Thurgood Marshall, 1987

> Thurgood Marshall (1908–1993) served as chief counsel for the American Association for the Advancement of Colored People before he was nominated to the Supreme Court of the United States in 1967. In the following speech, delivered on the two hundredth anniversary of the Constitutional Convention, Marshall considered the revolutionary principles proclaimed in the Declaration of Independence in light of the constitutional compromises involving slavery.

The year 1987 marks the 200th anniversary of the United States Constitution. A Commission has been established to coordinate the celebration. The official meetings, essay contests, and festivities have begun.

The planned commemoration will span three years, and I am told 1987 is "dedicated to the memory of the Founders and the document they drafted in Philadelphia." We are to "recall the achievements of our Founders and the knowledge and experience that inspired them, the nature of the government they established, its origins, its character and its ends, and the rights and privileges of citizenship, as well as its attendant responsibilities."

Like many anniversary celebrations, the plan for 1987 takes particular events and holds them up as the source of all the very best that has followed. Patriotic feelings will surely swell, prompting proud proclamations of the wisdom, foresight, and sense of justice shared by the framers and reflected in a written document now yellowed with age. This is unfortunate—not the patriotism itself, but the tendency for the celebration to oversimplify, and overlook the many other events that have been instrumental to our achievements as a nation. The focus of this celebration invites a complacent belief that the vision of those who debated and compromised in Philadelphia yielded the "more perfect Union" it is said we now enjoy.

I cannot accept this invitation, for I do not believe that the meaning of the Constitution was forever "fixed" at the Philadelphia Convention. Nor do I find the wisdom, foresight, and sense of justice exhibited by the framers particularly profound. To the contrary, the government they devised was defective from the start, requiring several amendments, a civil war, and momentous social transformation to attain the system of constitutional government, and its respect for the individual freedoms and human rights, that we hold as fundamental today. When contemporary Americans cite "The Constitution," they invoke a concept that is vastly different from what the framers barely began to construct two centuries ago.

For a sense of the evolving nature of the Constitution we need look no further than the first three words of the document's preamble: "We the People." When the Founding Fathers used this phrase in 1787, they did not have in mind the majority of America's citizens. "We the People" included, in the words of the framers, "the whole Number of free Persons." On a matter so basic as the right to vote, for example, Negro slaves were excluded, although they were counted for representational purposes—at three-fifths each. Women did not gain the right to vote for over a hundred and thirty years.

These omissions were intentional. The record of the framers' debates on the slave question is especially clear: the Southern states acceded to the demands of the New England states for giving Congress broad power to regulate commerce, in exchange for the right to continue the slave trade. The economic interests of the regions coalesced: New Englanders engaged in the "carrying trade" would profit from transporting slaves from Africa as well as goods produced in America by slave labor. The perpetuation of slavery ensured the primary source of wealth in the Southern states.

Despite this clear understanding of the role slavery would play in the new republic, use of the words "slaves" and "slavery" was carefully avoided in the original document. Political representation in the lower House of Congress was to be based on the population of "free Persons" in each state, plus three-fifths of all "other Persons." Moral principles against slavery, for those who had them, were compromised, with no explanation of the conflicting principles for which the American Revolutionary War had ostensibly been fought: the self-evident truths "that all men are created equal, that they are endowed by their Creator with certain unalienable Rights, that among these are Life, Liberty, and the pursuit of Happiness."

It was not the first such compromise. Even these ringing phrases from the Declaration of Independence are filled with irony, for an early draft of what became that declaration assailed the King of England for suppressing legislative attempts to end the slave trade and for encouraging slave rebellions. The final draft adopted in 1776 did not contain this criticism. And so again at the Constitutional Convention eloquent objections to the institution of slavery went unheeded, and its opponents eventually consented to a document which laid a foundation for the tragic events that were to follow.

Pennsylvania's Gouverneur Morris provides an example. He opposed slavery and the counting of slaves in determining the basis for representation in Congress. At the Convention he objected that

> The inhabitant of Georgia [or] South Carolina who goes to the coast of Africa, and in defiance of the most sacred laws of humanity tears away his fellow creatures from their dearest connections and damns them to the most cruel bondages, shall have more votes in a Government instituted for protection of the rights of mankind, than the Citizen of Pennsylvania or New Jersey who views with a laudable horror, so nefarious a practice.

And yet Governeur Morris eventually accepted the three-fifths accommodation. In fact, he wrote the final draft of the Constitution, the very document the bicentennial will commemorate.

As a result of compromise, the right of the Southern states to continue importing slaves was extended, officially, at least until 1808. We know that it actually lasted a good deal longer, as the framers possessed no monopoly on the ability to trade moral principles for self-interest. But they nevertheless set an unfortunate example. Slaves could be imported, if the commercial interests of the North were protected. To make the compromise even more palatable, customs duties would be imposed at up to ten dollars per slave as a means of raising public revenues.

No doubt it will be said, when the unpleasant truth of the history of slavery in America is mentioned during this bicentennial year, that the Constitution was a product of its times, and embodied a compromise which, under other circumstances, would not have been made. But the effects of the framers' compromise have remained for generations. They arose from the contradiction between guaranteeing liberty and justice to all, and denying both to Negroes.

The original intent of the phrase, "We the People,' was far too clear for any ameliorating construction. Writing for the Supreme Court in 1857, Chief Justice Taney penned the following passage in the *Dred Scott* case, on the issue of whether, in the eyes of the framers, slaves were "constituent members of the sovereignty," and were to be included among "We the People":

> We think they are not, and that they are not included, and were not intended to be included . . . .
> They had for more than a century before been regarded as beings of an inferior order, and altogether unfit to associate with the white race . . . ; and

so far inferior, that they had no rights which the white man was bound to respect; and that the negro might justly and lawfully be reduced to slavery for his benefit . . . .

. . . [A]ccordingly, a negro of the African race was regarded . . . as an article of property, and held, and bought and sold as such . . . . [N]o one seems to have doubted the correctness of the prevailing opinion of the time.

And so, nearly seven decades after the Constitutional Convention, the Supreme Court reaffirmed the prevailing opinion of the framers regarding the rights of Negroes in America. It took a bloody civil war before the thirteenth amendment could be adopted to abolish slavery, though not the consequences slavery would have for future Americans.

While the Union survived the civil war, the Constitution did not. In its place arose a new, more promising basis for justice and equality, the fourteenth amendment, ensuring protection of the life, liberty, and property of *all* persons against deprivations without due process, and guaranteeing equal protection of the laws. And yet almost another century would pass before any significant recognition was obtained of the rights of black Americans to share equally even in such basic opportunities as education, housing, and employment, and to have their votes counted, and counted equally. In the meantime, blacks joined America's military to fight its wars and invested untold hours working in its factories and on its farms, contributing to the development of this country's magnificent wealth and waiting to share in its prosperity.

What is striking is the role legal principles have played throughout America's history in determining the condition of Negroes. They were enslaved by law, emancipated by law, disenfranchised and segregated by law; and, finally, they have begun to win equality by law. Along the way, new constitutional principles have emerged to meet the challenges of a changing society. The progress has been dramatic, and it will continue.

The men who gathered in Philadelphia in 1787 could not have envisioned these changes. They could not have imagined, nor would they have accepted, that the document they were drafting would one day be construed by a Supreme Court to which had been appointed a woman and the descendent of an African slave. "We the People" no longer enslave, but the credit does not belong to the framers. It belongs to those who refused to acquiesce in outdated notions of "liberty," "justice," and "equality," and who strived to better them.

And so we must be careful, when focusing on the events which took place in Philadelphia two centuries ago, that we not overlook the momentous events which followed, and thereby lose our proper sense of perspective. Otherwise, the odds are that for many Americans the bicentennial celebration will be little more than a blind pilgrimage to the shrine of the original document now stored in a vault in the National Archives. If we seek, instead, a sensitive understanding of the Constitution's inherent defects, and its promising evolution through 200 years of history, the celebration of the "Miracle at Philadelphia" will, in my view, be a far more meaningful and humbling experience. We will see that the true miracle was not the birth of the Constitution, but its life: a life nurtured through two turbulent centuries of our own making, and a life embodying much good fortune that was not.

Thus, in this bicentennial year, we may not all participate in the festivities with flag-waving fervor. Some may more quietly commemorate the suffering, struggle, and sacrifice that has triumphed over much of what was wrong with the original document, and observe the anniversary with hopes not realized and promises not fulfilled. I plan to celebrate the bicentennial of the Constitution as a living document, including the Bill of Rights and the other amendments protecting individual freedoms and human rights.

31

The Sanctity of Human Life

Ronald Reagan, 1984

> *Ronald Reagan (1911–2004) served as the fortieth president of the United States, from 1981 to 1989. In 1984, Reagan declared January 22—the anniversary of the Supreme Court's landmark abortion rights decision in* Roe v. Wade *(1973)—to be National Sanctity of Human Life Day. In his proclamation, Reagan appealed to the principles of the Declaration of Independence and implied that abortion, like slavery, "mocked our dedication to the freedom and equality of all men and women."*

By the President of the United States of America
A Proclamation

The values and freedoms we cherish as Americans rest on our fundamental commitment to the sanctity of human life. The first of the "unalienable rights" affirmed by our Declaration of Independence is the right to life itself, a right the Declaration states has been endowed by our Creator on all human beings—whether young or old, weak or strong, healthy or handicapped.

Since 1973, however, more than 15 million unborn children have died in legalized abortions—a tragedy of stunning dimensions that stands in sad contrast to our belief that each life is sacred. These children, over tenfold the number of Americans lost in all our Nation's wars, will never laugh, never sing, never experience the joy of human love; nor will they strive to heal the sick, or feed the poor, or make peace among nations. Abortion has denied them the first and most basic of human rights, and we are infinitely poorer for their loss.

We are poorer not simply for lives not led and for contributions not made, but also for the erosion of our sense of the worth and dignity of every individual. To diminish the value of one category of human life is to diminish us all. Slavery, which treated Blacks as something less than human, to be bought and sold if convenient, cheapened human life and mocked our dedication to the freedom and equality of all men and women. Can we say that abortion—which treats the unborn as something less than human, to be destroyed if convenient—will be less corrosive to the values we hold dear?

We have been given the precious gift of human life, made more precious still by our births in or pilgrimages to a land of freedom. It is fitting, then, on the anniversary of the Supreme Court decision in Roe v. Wade that struck down State anti-abortion laws, that we reflect anew on these blessings, and on our corresponding responsibility to guard with care the lives and freedoms of even the weakest of our fellow human beings.

Now, Therefore, I, Ronald Reagan, President of the United States of America, do hereby proclaim Sunday, January 22, 1984, as National Sanctity of Human Life Day. I call upon the citizens of this blessed land to gather on that day in homes and places of worship to give thanks for the gift of life, and to reaffirm our commitment to the dignity of every human being and the sanctity of each human life.

In Witness Whereof, I have hereunto set my hand this 13th day of January, in the year of our Lord nineteen hundred and eighty-four, and of the Independence of the United States of America the two hundred and eighth.

Ronald Reagan

32

America's Work in the World

George W. Bush, 2003

Shortly after the U.S.-led invasion of Iraq in 2003, President George W. Bush (1946–) delivered the following Fourth of July speech at the United States Air Force Museum in Dayton, Ohio. In his remarks, Bush tied "America's work in the world" to the Declaration of Independence, which, he insisted, "holds a promise for all mankind."

... Every year on this date, we take special pride in the founding generation, the men and women who waged a desperate fight to overcome tyranny and live in freedom. Centuries later, it is hard to imagine the Revolutionary War coming out any way other than it—how it came out. Yet victory was far from certain, and came at great cost. Those brave men and women were certain only of the cause they served: the belief that freedom is the gift of God and the right of all mankind.

Six years passed from the fighting at Concord Bridge to the victory at Yorktown; six years of struggle and hardship for American patriots. By their courage and perseverance, the colonies became a country. The land of 13 states and fewer than four million people grew and prospered. And today, all who live in tyranny and all who yearn for freedom place their hopes in the United States of America.

For more than two centuries, Americans have been called to serve and sacrifice for the ideals of our founding. And the men and women of our military have never failed us. They have left many monuments along the way—an undivided union, a liberated Europe, the rise of democracy in Asia, and the fall of an evil empire. Millions across the world are free today because of the unselfish courage of American veterans. And today we honor our veterans.

And today we honor the current generation of our military, which is answering the call to defend our freedom and to bring freedom to others . . . Our United States military is meeting the threats of a new era. People in every branch of the service and thousands of Guard and reserve members called to active duty have carried out their missions with all the skill and honor we expect of them. This nation is grateful to the men and women who wear our nation's uniform.

And on this 4th of July, we also remember the brave Americans we have lost. We honor each one for their courage and for their service. We think of the families who miss them so much. And we are thankful that this nation produces such fine men and women who are willing to defend us all. May God rest their souls.

Our nation is still at war. The enemies of America plot against us. And many of our fellow citizens are still serving and sacrificing and facing danger in distant places. Many military families are separated. Our people in uniform do not have easy duty, and much depends on their success. Without America's active involvement in this world, the ambitions of tyrants would go unopposed, and millions would live at the mercy of terrorists. With Americans' active involvement in the world, tyrants learn to fear, and terrorists are on the run.

By killing innocent Americans, our enemies made their intentions clear to us. And since that September day, we have made our own intentions clear to them. The United States will not stand by and wait for another attack, or trust in the restraint and good intentions of evil men. We are on the offensive against terrorists and all who support them. We will not permit any terrorist group or outlaw regime to threaten us with weapons of mass murder. We will act whenever it is necessary to protect the lives and the liberty of the American people.

America's work in the world does not end with the removal of grave threats. The Declaration of Independence holds a promise for all mankind. Because Americans believe that freedom is an unalienable right, we value the freedom of every nation. Because we are committed to the God-given worth of every life, we work for human dignity. We protect our friends. And we raised up former enemies to be our friends.

We bring food and disaster relief to the nations of the world in times of crisis. In Africa, where I'll go next week, the United States is leading the effort to fight AIDS and save millions of lives with the healing power of medicine.

Just as our enemies are coming to know the strong will of America, people across the Earth are seeing the good and generous heart of America. Americans are a generous people because we realize how much we have been given. On the Fourth of July, we can be grateful for the unity of our country in meeting great challenges, for the renewal of patriotism that adversity has brought, and for the valor we have seen in those who defend the United States.

To be an American, whether by birth or choice, is a high privilege. As citizens of this good nation, we can all be proud of our heritage and confident in our future. The ideals of July 4th, 1776, still speak to all humanity. And the revolution declared that day goes on. On July 4th, 2003, we still place our trust in Divine Providence. We still pledge our lives and honor to freedom's defense. And we will always believe that freedom is the hope and the future of every land.

33

A More Perfect Union

Barack Obama, 2008

> During his presidential primary campaign in 2008, Barack Obama (1961–) gave a speech on American race relations at the National Constitution Center in Philadelphia, Pennsylvania. The speech was prompted, in part, by heightened media attention to racially inflammatory remarks made by Obama's then-pastor Jeremiah Wright. The Constitution of 1787, Obama declared in the speech, "finally made real" the promises of the Declaration of Independence, but the document was left incomplete because of the nation's "original sin of slavery."

"We the people, in order to form a more perfect union."

Two hundred and twenty one years ago, in a hall that still stands across the street, a group of men gathered and, with these simple words, launched America's improbable experiment in democracy. Farmers and scholars; statesmen and patriots who had traveled across an ocean to escape tyranny and persecution finally made real their declaration of independence at a Philadelphia convention that lasted through the spring of 1787. The document they produced was eventually signed but ultimately unfinished. It was stained by this nation's original sin of slavery, a question that divided the colonies and brought the convention to a stalemate until the founders chose to allow the slave trade to continue for at least twenty more years, and to leave any final resolution to future generations.

Of course, the answer to the slavery question was already embedded within our Constitution—a Constitution that had at is very core the ideal of equal citizenship under the law; a Constitution that promised its people liberty, and justice, and a union that could be and should be perfected over time.

And yet words on a parchment would not be enough to deliver slaves from bondage, or provide men and women of every color and creed their full rights and obligations as citizens of the United States. What would be needed were Americans in successive generations who were willing to do their part—through protests and struggle, on the streets and in the courts, through a civil war and civil disobedience and always at great risk—to narrow that gap between the promise of our ideals and the reality of their time.

This was one of the tasks we set forth at the beginning of this campaign—to continue the long march of those who came before us, a march for a more just, more equal, more free, more caring and more prosperous America. I chose to run for the presidency at this moment in history because I believe deeply that we cannot solve the challenges of our time unless we solve them together—unless we perfect our union by understanding that we may have different stories, but we hold common hopes; that we may not look the same and we may not have come from the same place, but we all want to move in the same direction—towards a better future for our children and our grandchildren.

This belief comes from my unyielding faith in the decency and generosity of the American people. But it also comes from my own American story.

I am the son of a black man from Kenya and a white woman from Kansas. I was raised with the help of a white grandfather who survived a Depression to serve in Patton's Army during World War II and a white grandmother who worked on a bomber assembly line at Fort Leavenworth while he was overseas. I've gone to some of the best schools in America and lived in one of the world's poorest nations. I am married to a black American who carries within her the blood of slaves and slaveowners—an inheritance we pass on to our two precious daughters. I have brothers, sisters, nieces, nephews, uncles and cousins, of every race and every hue, scattered across three continents, and for as long as I live, I will never forget that in no other country on Earth is my story even possible.

It's a story that hasn't made me the most conventional candidate. But it is a story that has seared into my genetic makeup the idea that this nation is more than the sum of its parts—that out of many, we are truly one.

Throughout the first year of this campaign, against all predictions to the contrary, we saw how hungry the American people were for this message of unity. Despite the temptation to view my candidacy through a purely racial lens, we won commanding victories in states with some of the whitest populations in the country. In South Carolina, where the Confederate Flag still flies, we built a powerful coalition of African Americans and white Americans.

This is not to say that race has not been an issue in the campaign. At various stages in the campaign, some commentators have deemed me either "too black" or "not black enough." We saw racial tensions bubble to the surface during the week before the South Carolina primary. The press has scoured every exit poll for the latest evidence of racial polarization, not just in terms of white and black, but black and brown as well.

And yet, it has only been in the last couple of weeks that the discussion of race in this campaign has taken a particularly divisive turn.

On one end of the spectrum, we've heard the implication that my candidacy is somehow an exercise in affirmative action; that it's based solely on the desire of wide-eyed liberals to purchase racial reconciliation on the cheap. On the other end, we've heard my former pastor, Reverend Jeremiah Wright, use incendiary language to express views that have the potential not only to widen the racial divide, but views that denigrate both the greatness and the goodness of our nation; that rightly offend white and black alike.

I have already condemned, in unequivocal terms, the statements of Reverend Wright that have caused such controversy. For some, nagging questions remain. Did I know him to be an occasionally fierce critic of American domestic and foreign policy? Of course. Did I ever hear him make remarks that could be considered controversial while I sat in church? Yes. Did I strongly disagree with many of his political views? Absolutely—just as I'm sure many of you have heard remarks from your pastors, priests, or rabbis with which you strongly disagreed.

But the remarks that have caused this recent firestorm weren't simply controversial. They weren't simply a religious leader's effort to speak out against perceived injustice. Instead, they expressed a profoundly distorted view of this country—a view that sees white racism as endemic, and that elevates what is wrong with America above all that we know is right with America; a view that sees the conflicts in the Middle East as rooted primarily in the actions of stalwart allies like Israel, instead of emanating from the perverse and hateful ideologies of radical Islam.

As such, Reverend Wright's comments were not only wrong but divisive, divisive at a time when we need unity; racially charged at a time when we need to come together to solve a set of monumental problems—two wars, a terrorist threat, a falling economy, a chronic health care crisis and potentially devastating climate change; problems that are neither black or white or Latino or Asian, but rather problems that confront us all.

Given my background, my politics, and my professed values and ideals, there will no doubt be those for whom my statements of condemnation are not enough. Why associate myself with Reverend Wright in the first place, they may ask? Why not join another church? And I confess that if all that I knew of Reverend Wright were the snippets of those sermons that have run in an endless loop on the television and YouTube, or if Trinity United Church of Christ conformed to the caricatures being peddled by some commentators, there is no doubt that I would react in much the same way.

But the truth is, that isn't all that I know of the man. The man I met more than twenty years ago is a man who helped introduce me to my Christian faith, a man who spoke to me about our obligations to love one another; to care for the sick and lift up the poor. He is a man who served his country as a U.S. Marine; who has studied and lectured at some of the finest universities and seminaries in the country, and who for over thirty years led a church that serves the community by doing God's work here on Earth—by housing the homeless, ministering to the needy, providing day care services and scholarships and prison ministries, and reaching out to those suffering from HIV/AIDS.

In my first book, *Dreams From My Father*, I described the experience of my first service at Trinity:

> People began to shout, to rise from their seats and clap and cry out, a forceful wind carrying the reverend's voice up into the rafters....And in that single note—hope!—I heard something else; at the foot of that cross, inside the thousands of churches across the city, I imagined the stories of ordinary black people merging with the stories of David and Goliath, Moses and Pharaoh, the Christians in the lion's den, Ezekiel's field of dry bones. Those stories—of survival, and freedom, and hope—became our story, my story; the blood that had spilled was our blood, the tears our tears; until this black church, on this bright day, seemed once more a vessel carrying the story of a people into future generations and into a larger world. Our trials and triumphs became at once unique and universal, black and more than black; in chronicling our journey, the stories and songs gave us a means to reclaim memories that we didn't need to feel shame about...memories that all people might study and cherish—and with which we could start to rebuild.

That has been my experience at Trinity. Like other predominantly black churches across the country, Trinity embodies the black community in its entirety—the doctor and the welfare mom, the model student and the former gang-banger. Like other black churches, Trinity's services are full of raucous laughter and sometimes bawdy humor. They are full of dancing, clapping, screaming and shouting that may seem jarring to the untrained ear. The church contains in full the kindness and cruelty, the fierce intelligence and the shocking ignorance, the struggles and successes, the love and yes, the bitterness and bias that make up the black experience in America.

And this helps explain, perhaps, my relationship with Reverend Wright. As imperfect as he may be, he has been like family to me. He strengthened my faith, officiated my wedding, and baptized my children. Not once in my conversations with him have I heard him talk about any ethnic group in derogatory terms, or treat whites with whom he interacted with anything but courtesy and respect. He contains within him the contradictions—the good and the bad—of the community that he has served diligently for so many years.

I can no more disown him than I can disown the black community. I can no more disown him than I can my white grandmother—a woman who helped raise me, a woman who sacrificed again and again for me, a woman who loves me as much as she loves anything in this world, but a woman who once confessed her fear of black men who passed by her on the street, and who on more than one occasion has uttered racial or ethnic stereotypes that made me cringe.

These people are a part of me. And they are a part of America, this country that I love.

Some will see this as an attempt to justify or excuse comments that are simply inexcusable. I can assure you it is not. I suppose the politically safe thing would be to move on from this episode and just hope that it fades into the woodwork. We can dismiss Reverend Wright as a crank or a demagogue, just as some have dismissed Geraldine Ferraro, in the aftermath of her recent statements, as harboring some deep-seated racial bias.

But race is an issue that I believe this nation cannot afford to ignore right now. We would be making the same mistake that Reverend Wright made in his offending sermons about America—to simplify and stereotype and amplify the negative to the point that it distorts reality.

The fact is that the comments that have been made and the issues that have surfaced over the last few weeks reflect the complexities of race in this country that we've never really worked through—a part of our union that we have yet to perfect. And if we walk away now, if we simply retreat into our respective corners, we will never be able to come together and solve challenges like health care, or education, or the need to find good jobs for every American.

Understanding this reality requires a reminder of how we arrived at this point. As William Faulkner once wrote, "The past isn't dead and buried. In fact, it isn't even past." We do not need to recite here the history of racial injustice in this country. But we do need to remind ourselves that so many of the disparities that exist in the African-American community today can be directly traced to inequalities passed on from an earlier generation that suffered under the brutal legacy of slavery and Jim Crow.

Segregated schools were, and are, inferior schools; we still haven't fixed them, fifty years after *Brown v. Board of Education*, and the inferior education they provided, then and now, helps explain the pervasive achievement gap between today's black and white students.

Legalized discrimination—where blacks were prevented, often through violence, from owning property, or loans were not granted to African-American business owners, or black homeowners could not access FHA mortgages, or blacks were excluded from unions, or the police force, or fire departments—meant that black families could not amass any meaningful wealth to bequeath to future generations. That history helps explain the wealth and income gap between black and white, and the concentrated pockets of poverty that persists in so many of today's urban and rural communities.

A lack of economic opportunity among black men, and the shame and frustration that came from not being able to provide for one's family, contributed to the erosion of black families—a problem that welfare policies for many years may have worsened. And the lack of basic services in so many urban black neighborhoods—parks for kids to play in, police walking the beat, regular garbage pick-up and building code enforcement—all helped create a cycle of violence, blight and neglect that continue to haunt us.

This is the reality in which Reverend Wright and other African-Americans of his generation grew up. They came of age in the late fifties and early sixties, a time when segregation was still the law of the land and opportunity was systematically constricted. What's remarkable is not how many failed in the face of discrimination, but rather how many men and women overcame the odds; how many were able to make a way out of no way for those like me who would come after them.

But for all those who scratched and clawed their way to get a piece of the American Dream, there were many who didn't make it—those who were ultimately defeated, in one way or another, by discrimination. That legacy of defeat was passed on to future generations—those young men and increasingly young women who we see standing on street corners or languishing in our prisons, without hope or prospects for the future. Even for those blacks who did make it, questions of race, and racism, continue to define their worldview in fundamental ways. For the men and women of Reverend Wright's generation, the memories of humiliation and doubt and fear have not gone away; nor has the anger and the bitterness of those years. That anger may not get expressed in public, in front of white co-workers or white friends. But it does find voice in the barbershop or around the kitchen table. At times, that anger is exploited by politicians, to gin up votes along racial lines, or to make up for a politician's own failings.

And occasionally it finds voice in the church on Sunday morning, in the pulpit and in the pews. The fact that so many people are surprised to hear that anger in some of Reverend Wright's sermons simply reminds us of the old truism that the most segregated hour in American life occurs on Sunday morning. That anger is not always productive; indeed, all too often it distracts attention from solving real problems; it keeps us from squarely facing our own complicity in our condition, and prevents the African-American community from forging the alliances it needs to bring about real change. But the anger is real; it is powerful; and to simply wish it away, to condemn it without understanding its roots, only serves to widen the chasm of misunderstanding that exists between the races.

In fact, a similar anger exists within segments of the white community. Most working- and middle-class white Americans don't feel that they have been particularly privileged by their race. Their experience is the immigrant experience—as far as they're concerned, no one's handed them anything, they've built it from scratch. They've worked hard all their lives, many times only to see their jobs shipped overseas or their pension dumped after a lifetime of labor. They are anxious about their futures, and feel their dreams slipping away; in an era of stagnant wages and global competition, opportunity comes to be seen as a zero sum game, in which your dreams come at my expense. So when they are told to bus their children to a school across town; when they hear that an African American is getting an advantage in landing a good job or a spot in a good college because of an injustice that they themselves never committed; when they're told that their fears about crime in urban neighborhoods are somehow prejudiced, resentment builds over time.

Like the anger within the black community, these resentments aren't always expressed in polite company. But they have helped shape the political landscape for at least a generation. Anger over welfare and affirmative action helped forge the Reagan Coalition. Politicians routinely exploited fears of crime for their own electoral ends. Talk show hosts and conservative commentators built entire careers unmasking bogus claims of racism while dismissing legitimate discussions of racial injustice and inequality as mere political correctness or reverse racism.

Just as black anger often proved counterproductive, so have these white resentments distracted attention from the real culprits of the middle class squeeze—a corporate culture rife with inside dealing, questionable accounting practices, and short-term greed; a Washington dominated by lobbyists and special interests; economic policies that favor the few over the many. And yet, to wish away the resentments of white Americans, to label them as misguided or even racist, without recognizing they are grounded in legitimate concerns—this too widens the racial divide, and blocks the path to understanding.

This is where we are right now. It's a racial stalemate we've been stuck in for years. Contrary to the claims of some of my critics, black and white, I have never been so naïve as to believe that we can get beyond our racial divisions in a single election cycle, or with a single candidacy—particularly a candidacy as imperfect as my own.

But I have asserted a firm conviction—a conviction rooted in my faith in God and my faith in the American people—that working together we can move beyond some of our old racial wounds, and that in fact we have no choice if we are to continue on the path of a more perfect union.

For the African-American community, that path means embracing the burdens of our past without becoming victims of our past. It means continuing to insist on a full measure of justice in every aspect of American life. But it also means binding our particular grievances—for better health care, and better schools, and better jobs—to the larger aspirations of all Americans—the white woman struggling to break the glass ceiling, the white man whose been laid off, the immigrant trying to feed his family. And it means taking full responsibility for own lives—by demanding more from our fathers, and spending more time with our children, and reading to them, and teaching them that while they may face challenges and discrimination in their own lives, they must never succumb to despair or cynicism; they must always believe that they can write their own destiny.

Ironically, this quintessentially American—and yes, conservative—notion of self-help found frequent expression in Reverend Wright's sermons. But what my former pastor too often failed to understand is that embarking on a program of self-help also requires a belief that society can change.

The profound mistake of Reverend Wright's sermons is not that he spoke about racism in our society. It's that he spoke as if our society was static; as if no progress has been made; as if this country—a country that has made it possible for one of his own members to run for the highest office in the land and build a coalition of white and black; Latino and Asian, rich and poor, young and old—is still irrevocably bound to a tragic past. But what we know—what we have seen—is that America can change. That is the true genius of this nation. What we have already achieved gives us hope—the audacity to hope—for what we can and must achieve tomorrow.

In the white community, the path to a more perfect union means acknowledging that what ails the African-American community does not just exist in the minds of black people; that the legacy of discrimination—and current incidents of discrimination, while less overt than in the past—are real and must be addressed. Not just with words, but with deeds—by investing in our schools and our communities; by enforcing our civil rights laws and ensuring fairness in our criminal justice system; by providing this generation with ladders of opportunity that were unavailable for previous generations. It requires all Americans to realize that your dreams do not have to come at the expense of my dreams; that investing in the health, welfare, and education of black and brown and white children will ultimately help all of America prosper.

In the end, then, what is called for is nothing more, and nothing less, than what all the world's great religions demand—that we do unto others as we would have them do unto us. Let us be our brother's keeper, Scripture tells us. Let us be our sister's keeper. Let us find that common stake we all have in one another, and let our politics reflect that spirit as well.

For we have a choice in this country. We can accept a politics that breeds division, and conflict, and cynicism. We can tackle race only as spectacle—as we did in the OJ trial—or in the wake of tragedy, as we did in the aftermath of Katrina— or as fodder for the nightly news. We can play Reverend Wright's sermons on every channel, every day and talk about them from now until the election, and make the only question in this campaign whether or not the American people think that I somehow believe or sympathize with his most offensive words. We can pounce on some gaffe by a Hillary supporter as evidence that she's playing the race card, or we can speculate on whether white men will all flock to John McCain in the general election regardless of his policies.

We can do that.

But if we do, I can tell you that in the next election, we'll be talking about some other distraction. And then another one. And then another one. And nothing will change.

That is one option. Or, at this moment, in this election, we can come together and say, "Not this time." This time we want to talk about the crumbling schools that are stealing the future of black children and white children and Asian children and Hispanic children and Native American children. This time we want to reject the cynicism that tells us that these kids can't learn; that those kids who don't look like us are somebody else's problem. The children of America are not those kids, they are our kids, and we will not let them fall behind in a 21st century economy. Not this time.

This time we want to talk about how the lines in the Emergency Room are filled with whites and blacks and Hispanics who do not have health care; who don't have the power on their own to overcome the special interests in Washington, but who can take them on if we do it together.

This time we want to talk about the shuttered mills that once provided a decent life for men and women of every race, and the homes for sale that once belonged to Americans from every religion, every region, every walk of life. This time we want to talk about the fact that the real problem is not that someone who doesn't look like you might take your job; it's that the corporation you work for will ship it overseas for nothing more than a profit.

This time we want to talk about the men and women of every color and creed who serve together, and fight together, and bleed together under the same proud flag. We want to talk about how to bring them home from a war that never should've been authorized and never should've been waged, and we want to talk about how we'll show our patriotism by caring for them, and their families, and giving them the benefits they have earned.

I would not be running for President if I didn't believe with all my heart that this is what the vast majority of Americans want for this country. This union may never be perfect, but generation after generation has shown that it can always be perfected. And today, whenever I find myself feeling doubtful or cynical about this possibility, what gives me the most hope is the next generation—the young people whose attitudes and beliefs and openness to change have already made history in this election.

There is one story in particular that I'd like to leave you with today—a story I told when I had the great honor of speaking on Dr. King's birthday at his home church, Ebenezer Baptist, in Atlanta.

There is a young, twenty-three year old white woman named Ashley Baia who organized for our campaign in Florence, South Carolina. She had been working to organize a mostly African-American community since the beginning of this campaign, and one day she was at a roundtable discussion where everyone went around telling their story and why they were there.

And Ashley said that when she was nine years old, her mother got cancer. And because she had to miss days of work, she was let go and lost her health care. They had to file for bankruptcy, and that's when Ashley decided that she had to do something to help her mom.

She knew that food was one of their most expensive costs, and so Ashley convinced her mother that what she really liked and really wanted to eat more than anything else was mustard and relish sandwiches. Because that was the cheapest way to eat.

She did this for a year until her mom got better, and she told everyone at the roundtable that the reason she joined our campaign was so that she could help the millions of other children in the country who want and need to help their parents too.

Now Ashley might have made a different choice. Perhaps somebody told her along the way that the source of her mother's problems were blacks who were on welfare and too lazy to work, or Hispanics who were coming into the country illegally. But she didn't. She sought out allies in her fight against injustice.

Anyway, Ashley finishes her story and then goes around the room and asks everyone else why they're supporting the campaign. They all have different stories and reasons. Many bring up a specific issue. And finally they come to this elderly black man who's been sitting there quietly the entire time. And Ashley asks him why he's there. And he does not bring up a specific issue. He does not say health care or the economy. He does not say education or the war. He does not say that he was there because of Barack Obama. He simply says to everyone in the room, "I am here because of Ashley."

"I'm here because of Ashley." By itself, that single moment of recognition between that young white girl and that old black man is not enough. It is not enough to give health care to the sick, or jobs to the jobless, or education to our children.

But it is where we start. It is where our union grows stronger. And as so many generations have come to realize over the course of the two-hundred and twenty one years since a band of patriots signed that document in Philadelphia, that is where the perfection begins.

Notes

FOREWORD

(David Boren is President of the University of Oklahoma. He served previously as Governor of Oklahoma and as a United States Senator where he was the longest serving chairman of the Select Committee on Intellegence. Boren, a Rhodes Scholar has degrees from Yale (BA summa cum laude), Oxford University (MA) and the University of Oklahoma College of Law (JD).)

1. Intercollegiate Studies Institute Report, 2000.
2. San Diego Union, November 2, 2002.
3 American Council of Trustees and Alumni, February 21, 2000.
4. College Board Report, 2010.

INTRODUCTION

1. John Adams, "Letter to Abigail Adams" (July 3, 1776) in John Adams, *The Works of John Adams, Second President of the United States: With a Life of the Author, Notes and Illustrations, by his Grandson Charles Francis Adams* (Boston: Little, Brown and Co., 1856). 10 volumes. Vol. 9. Chapter: TO MRS. ADAMS.

2. Resolution introduced in the Continental Congress by Richard Henry Lee (Virginia) Proposing a Declaration of Independence, June 7, 1776. http://avalon.law.yale.edu/18th_century/lee asp

3. Ibid., 301–2.

4. Carl Becker, *The Declaration of Independence: A Study in the History of Political Ideas* (New York: Harcourt, Brace, and Co., 1922), 277–78.

5. G. K. Chesterton, *What I Saw in America* (New York Dodd, Mead, and Co., 1922), 305.

6. Ibid., 308.

7. Carl Becker, *The Declaration of Independence: A Study in the History of Political Ideas*, 8th ed. (New York: Alfred A. Knopf, [1922] 1964).

8. Abraham Lincoln, "Fragment on the Constitution and the Union," (January 1861) in Roy P. Basler, *Collected Works of Abraham Lincoln* (New Brunswick, NJ: Rutgers University Press, 1953), 4:169. Cf. Proverbs 25:11.

9. Abraham Lincoln, "Fifth Debate with Stephen A. Douglas at Galesburg, Illinois" (October 7, 1858) in Roy P. Basler, *Collected Works of Abraham Lincoln* (New Brunswick, NJ: Rutgers University Press, 1953), 3:234.

10. Abraham Lincoln, "Gettysburg Address," in Roy P. Basler, *Collected Works of Abraham Lincoln* (New Brunswick, NJ: Rutgers University Press, 1953), 7:21.

11. Martin Luther King Jr., "I Have a Dream" (speech delivered August 28, 1963) at the Lincoln Memorial, Washington, D.C.

12. Barack Obama, "Speech at the Constitution Center," Philadelphia, March 18, 2008.

CHAPTER 1

Journals of the Continental Congress, 1774-1789, ed. Worthington C. Ford, et al. (Washington, DC, 1904–1937), 5:510–15.

CHAPTER 2

This reconstruction is based on Thomas Jefferson's original rough draft in Thomas Jefferson Randolph, ed., *Memoirs, Correspondence, and Private Papers of Thomas Jefferson*, 4 vols. (Charlottesville, 1829), 1:16–21.

CHAPTER 3

Letter from John Adams to Abigail Adams, 3 July 1776, "Your Favour of June 17 . . . "; Letter from John Adams to Abigail Adams, 3 July 1776, "Had a Declaration. . . . " Original manuscripts are housed in the Adams Family Papers, Massachusetts Historical Society.

CHAPTER 4

Jeremy Bentham, "A Short Review of the Declaration," in Jeremy Bentham and John Lind, *An Answer to the Declaration of the American Congress* (London: T. Cadell, J. Walter, and T. Sewell, 1776), 119–32.

CHAPTER 5

Letter of Thomas Jefferson to Richard Henry Lee, May 8, 1825, The Exhibition of Thomas Jefferson, the Library of Congress (www.loc.gov/exhibits/jefferson/jeffleg.html).

CHAPTER 6

Jonathan Elliot, ed., *The Debates in the Several State Conventions on the Adoption of the Federal Constitution as Recommended by the General Convention at Philadelphia in 1787*, 5 vols. (New York: Burt Franklin, 1888), 2:4888-850.

CHAPTER 7

Daniel Webster, *An Anniversary Address, Delivered Before the Federal Gentlemen of Concord . . . July 4th, 1806* (Concord, NH: George Hough, 1806).

CHAPTER 8

Lemuel Shaw, *An Oration, Delivered at Boston, July 4, 1815 . . . In Commemoration of American Independence* (Boston: John Eliot, 1815).

CHAPTER 9

John Quincy Adams, *An Address Delivered at the Request of a Committee of the Citizens of Washington: On the Occasion of Reading the Declaration of Independence* (Washington, D.C.: Davis & Force, 1821)

CHAPTER 10

Letter of Thomas Jefferson to Roger Weightman, 24 June 1826, The exhibition of Thomas Jefferson, the Library of Congress (www.loc.gov/exhibits/jefferson/214.html).

CHAPTER 11

William Wirt, *A Discourse on the Lives and Characters of Thomas Jefferson and John Adams* (Washington, D.C.: Gales & Seaton, 1826).

CHAPTER 12

Petition for Freedom to the Massachusetts Council and the House of Representatives, 13 January 1777. Jeremy Belknap papers, Massachusetts Historical Society.

CHAPTER 13

Max Farrand, *The Records of the Federal Convention of 1787*, 3 vols. (New Haven, CT: Yale University Press, 1911), 3: 210–13.

CHAPTER 14

William Lloyd Garrison, "An Address Delivered in Marlboro Chapel, Boston, July 4, 1838" (Boston: Isaac Knapp, 1838).

CHAPTER 15

John Quincy Adams, *Argument of John Quincy Adams Before the Supreme Court of the United States in the Case of the United States, Appellants, vs. Cinque, and others, Africans, Captured in the Schooner Amistad, by Lieut. Gedney, Delivered on the 25th of February and 1st of March 1841* (New York: S. W. Benedict, 1841).

CHAPTER 16

Senator John C. Calhoun, *Congressional Globe*, 30th Congress, 1st Session (June 27, 1848), appendix pp. 868–69.

CHAPTER 17

Frederick Douglass, *Oration, Delivered in Corinthian Hall, Rochester, by Frederick Douglass, July 5th*, 1852 (Rochester, NY: Lee, Mann & Co., 1852).

CHAPTER 18

The Official Proceedings of the 1856 Republican National Convention, Philadelphia, Pennsylvania, June 17–19, 1856.

CHAPTER 19

Dred Scott v. Sandford, 60 U.S. 393 (1857).

CHAPTER 20

"First Debate with Stephen A. Douglas at Ottawa, Illinois," in Roy P. Basler, *Collected Works of Abraham Lincoln* (New Brunswick: Rutgers University Press, 1953), 3: 1–37.

CHAPTER 21

Henry Cleveland, *Alexander H. Stephens, in Public and Private: With Letters and Speeches, Before, During, and Since the Civil War* (Philadelphia, 1886), 717–29.

CHAPTER 22

Abraham Lincoln, "Gettysburg Address," in Roy P. Basler, *Collected Works of Abraham Lincoln* (New Brunswick, NJ: Rutgers University Press 1953), 7:21.

CHAPTER 23

Rep. James Wilson (R-IA), *Congressional Globe*, 38th Congress, 1st Session, 1864, 1202–203; Rep. Ignatius Donnelly (R-MN); *Congressional Globe*, 39th Congress, 1st Session, 1866, 588;
Rep. John Bingham (R-MI), *Congressional Globe*, 39th Congress, 1st Session, 1866, 1291; Sen. Lyman Trumbull (R-IL), *Congressional Globe*, 39th Congress, 1st Session, 1866, 1757; Sen. Jacob Howard (R-MI), *Congressional Globe*, 39th Congress 1st Session, 1866, 2765.

CHAPTER 24

Report of the Woman's Rights Convention, N.Y., Held at Seneca Falls, July 19th and 20th, 1848 (Rochester, 1848).

CHAPTER 25

Circular, National Woman Suffrage Association, *Declaration of Rights of the Women of the United States . . . July 4th, 1876* (N.p., n.d.).

CHAPTER 26

Carrie Chapman Catt, *An Address to the Congress of the United States by Carrie Chapman Catt, President of the National American Woman Suffrage Association*. (New York: National American Woman Suffrage Publishing, 1917).

CHAPTER 27

Woodrow Wilson, *The New Freedom* (New York: Doubleday, Page, and Company, 1913), 33–54.

CHAPTER 28

Calvin Coolidge, Address on the One Hundred and Fiftieth Anniversary of the Declaration of Independence, Philadelphia, July 5, 1926. In James D. Richardson, comp., *Supplement to the Messages and Papers of the Presidents Covering the Second Administration of Calvin Coolidge* . . . (New York: Bureau of National Literature, 1929), 22: 9575–583.

CHAPTER 29

Franklin Roosevelt, Campaign Address on Progressive Government at the Commonwealth Club, San Francisco, CA, September 23, 1932. In *Public Papers of Franklin Delano Roosevelt* (New York: Random House, 1938), 1: 742–45.

CHAPTER 30

Thurgood Marshall, speech delivered at the Annual Seminar of the San Francisco Patent and Trademark Law Association in Maui, Hawaii, on May 6, 1987.

CHAPTER 31

Ronald Reagan, "National Sanctity of Human Life Day in January 13, 1984." The Public Papers of President Ronald W. Reagan. Ronald Reagan Presidential Library. (www.reagan.utexas.edu/archives/speeches/1984/11384c.htm)

CHAPTER 32

George W. Bush, July 4, 2003. Office of the Press Secretary.

CHAPTER 33

Barack Obama, "Speech at the Constitution Center," Philadelphia, March 18, 2008.

Index

Articles of Confederation, 90

Becker, Carl, xvi
Bible, 59, 64, 86, 96, 120, 146
Blackstone, William, 20, 89, 95

Chesterton, G. K., xvi
Christianity, 43, 49, 65, 67, 75, 77, 87, 141–42
citizenship, xviii, 71–72, 74–76, 85, 98, 104, 129, 139
Civil War, 83, 85, 130, 132, 140
conscience, 27, 66, 95
Constitution, United States, 22–24, 26, 28–29, 55, 60, 79–80, 90, 99, 101, 107–8, 113, 116, 119, 127; and the Declaration of Independence, xvii, xviii, 68; and slavery, xvii, 45–48, 64, 69, 70–73, 76, 86, 87, 129–33, 139
Creator, xv, 3, 7, 21, 50, 56, 60, 81, 81–2, 93, 96, 122, 127, 130, 134. *See also* God; Judge; Providence

Darwin, Charles, 107–8
democracy, xvi, 104, 106, 117, 118–19, 122, 136, 139

Dred Scott v. *Sandford* (1857), xvii, 70–73, 131; in Lincoln-Douglas debates, 74–8
due process, 69, 132

equal protection, 85, 132
equality, xvi, 51–52, 61–62, 66, 73–78, 80, 81, 88–89, 93, 96–97, 99–100, 102, 104, 111, 116–19, 126, 132, 134, 135

The Federalist, 108
Fourteenth Amendment, 132

God, ix, xv, 13, 15–18, 22, 24, 29, 30, 34, 35, 38, 40, 46, 49–52, 55, 63–67, 75, 84, 85–86, 88, 95, 108, 114, 116–18, 136–37, 145; Nature's, 3, 7, 16–17, 32, 54, 93, 108, 117. *See also* Creator; Judge; Providence

habeas corpus, 90, 99
happiness, the pursuit of, xv, xviii, 3, 7, 17, 18, 21, 27, 50, 51, 56, 68, 78, 86, 90, 93, 121, 128, 130, 134
human nature, 10, 32, 96, 102, 113

Jefferson, Thomas, xii, xv, xvi, xviii, 7, 19, 34, 36–9, 51, 62, 68, 79, 80, 85, 108, 117, 123–24, 128
Judge, God as the supreme, 6, 11, 117

Kansas–Nebraska Act, 68–69
King, Martin Luther Jr., xvii, 148

laws of nature, 3, 7, 16, 17, 32, 43, 79, 80, 81, 93, 108
liberty, natural right to, xv, 3, 21, 50, 51, 52, 56, 61, 93, 130, 134
life, natural right to, xv, 3, 7, 21, 50, 56, 68, 78, 93, 127, 130, 134
Lincoln, Abraham, xvii, 74–78, 83–84, 103
Locke, John, 19, 21, 60

Magna Carta, 79
Missouri Compromise, 59, 68–9
Montesquieu, Baron de, 108
morality, principles of, xvii, 24, 31, 36, 38, 60–1, 65, 67, 73, 78, 80, 94–96, 100–1, 120, 130
Morris, Governeur, 131

natural law. *See* laws of nature
natural rights, xvi, xvii, 78, 87, 89, 99, 102, 117
Newton, Isaac, 107–8
Northwest Ordinance, 58, 62

patriotism, 24, 27, 61, 98, 104, 129, 137, 147
popular sovereignty, 20, 76–77, 117–18

property, rights of private, 10, 27, 53, 55–57, 69, 73, 76, 79, 89, 90, 94, 97, 100–1, 123–24, 126–28, 132, 143
Providence, 6, 11, 14, 27, 32, 80, 81, 117, 138. *See also* Creator; God; Judge
Pufendorf, Samuel, 116

religion, 24, 43, 67, 86, 96, 113, 116–18, 146–47
religious liberty, 39, 7
Republican Party, 68–69, 75–77, 125
republicanism, 47, 67, 87
Roe v. Wade (1973), 134–35

Scripture. *See* Bible
self-government, 35, 77–8, 98, 101–2, 118–19
September 11, terrorist attacks on, 137
sex (gender), 5, 10, 50, 99–102, 103–6
slavery, xvii, xviii, 10, 43–44, 45–48, 49–52, 53–57, 58–62, 63–67, 68–69, 70–73, 74–78, 79–82, 85–8, 101, 129–33, 134–35, 139–40, 143
suffrage, women's, xviii, 93–7, 98–102, 103–6

Taney, Roger B., xvii, 131
taxation, 24, 50, 99, 100, 103, 104
Thirteenth Amendment, 132

Whitefield, George, 117
Wise, John, 116–17, 119
World War II, xvi, 140
Wright, Jeremiah, 141–44, 146

About the Author

Justin Buckley Dyer is assistant professor of political science at the University of Missouri–Columbia and the author of *Natural Law and the Antislavery Constitutional Tradition*.

www.ingramcontent.com/pod-product-compliance
Lightning Source LLC
Chambersburg PA
CBHW030113010526
44116CB00005B/233